Icarus World Issues Series

Apartheid
Calibrations of Color

Series Editors, Roger Rosen and Patra McSharry

THE ROSEN PUBLISHING GROUP, INC.
NEW YORK

Published in 1991 by The Rosen Publishing Group, Inc.
29 East 21st Street, New York, NY 10010

First Edition

Library of Congress Cataloging-in Publication Data

Apartheid : calibrations of color. -- 1st ed.
      p.   cm.   -- (Icarus world issues series)
      Includes bibliographical references and index.
      Summary: Essays, fiction, and photographs address different aspects of apartheid.
      ISBN 0-8239-1330-9 (hardcover)
          0-8239-1331-7 (paperback)
  1. Apartheid--Juvenile literature. [1. Apartheid.]
    I. Series.
DT1757.A62 1991
305.8--dc20   91-9905
                                    CIP
                                    AC

Manufactured in the United States of America

CONTENTS

Preface

Originally, the word "apartheid" simply meant "separateness" in Afrikaans, the language that came into existence as a hybrid of the Dutch, French, and German spoken by South Africa's European settlers. Afrikaans was also the language of command shared by Afrikaner settlers and the slaves imported to the Colony from the Dutch East Indies. Although these groups were separated, they were also thrown together, locked in combat and embrace. As the Colony grew, so too did a new population of mixed race, the so-called "Coloreds." When the borders eventually expanded to encompass the Black peoples of southern Africa, the conflict and mixing continued. While Afrikaans became for many the language of the oppressor, even today it is the mother tongue in which many of mixed race voice their opposition to apartheid.

Apartheid is a political philosophy devised by the Afrikaner Nationalist Party, which has been in power since 1948. The party's first action was to remove the limited voting rights that the British, during their rule of South Africa, had allowed Black and Colored citizens. The theory of apartheid was that each cultural group was to be kept separate, preserving its language, customs, and identity. That guaranteed Afrikaners the recognition and preservation of their language, free from the English control against which they had fought violently for centuries. Above all, this careful manipulation of ethnic categories by the architects of apartheid was designed to ensure that power stayed in the hands of White South Africans.

Apartheid effectively scattered South Africa's vast Black majority into "tribal" minorities, each banished to a barren "homeland" in which they could theoretically voice their political concerns in their own language on their designated scrap of land. In that way the Black majority, 80% of the population, was allocated 13% of the land, while "Coloreds" and "Asians" from India received neither land nor representation. This separation of groups could not hide the fact of their shared oppression and lack of any voice in the organization and control of the vast territory that became White South Africa. The resistance they had always expressed intensified under apartheid.

If you say "apart-hide," South Africans chuckle. They all pronounce it "apart-hate." Although merely a coincidence of pronunciation, what could be more appropriate when Afrikaans is the language associated with a system that has kept races apart and produced such hatred? Part of their amusement is also bemusement, because this little difference in speech is symbolic of the gulf of difference that separates those who live under apartheid and those who experience it secondhand through television and the press. Apartheid is not simply a Black and White issue, as outsiders tend to see it. There are Whites who fight apartheid, and Blacks who support it.

Other important resonances are hidden in the words South Africans use. Words mean different things, depending on who uses them. For example, when the South African government says "Black" it refers to those of African "tribal" origin. "Tribe" is a word that wounds like a knife, because "tribal" difference has been the official criterion of separation that has carved up the land and segregated peoples. On the other hand, when opponents of apartheid say "Black" they mean all South Africans of color, including "Indians" and all who fall into one of the seven classifications of "Coloreds." They are also quick to point out that it doesn't matter whether "Black" becomes ambiguous and includes various groups because the struggle is against racism and ethnic classifications. It is a multiracial battle, including Whites.

As to Shakespeare's question, What's in a name?, South

Africans will tell you that every surname pointedly hints at the color, race, and ethnicity of your father. Every name on the map of South Africa suggests a history tied to one group or another. As you begin to discern the "hate" hidden in apartheid, you come to understand how battles can break out over words, how names can become battlefields, and how it was that a struggle over language ignited a wave of protest that continues to resonate throughout South Africa.

By 1976 the Black schoolchildren of Soweto had had enough of the inferior education that circumscribed their futures. They knew that apartheid education provided each Black student with about one-tenth the subsidy given each White child. However, the final straw was the government's attempt to make Afrikaans instead of English the medium of education in Soweto schools. Black students recognized this as another means of disfranchisement intended to perpetuate their servitude to Afrikaners and prevent their connection with and understanding of the outside world. Soweto exploded, and soon protest spread throughout the country. Although the government tried to quench the flames, the resistance sparked by Soweto schoolchildren has burned steadily ever since.

Before European colonization, African literature consisted of oral traditions passed from generation to generation, with dynamic changes and embellishments depending on varying circumstances. When Europeans arrived with books, Africans were horrified at this method of freezing ideas and stories for all time and imposing them on succeeding generations. For Africans, the fitting end for books and art was the freedom of decay.

In all countries where aggressive colonization has taken place, it is the colonizer's language, economics, and technology that have come to dominate. In order to fight back, or even to be heard, the other has usually been forced to do so in the colonizer's terms. For South Africans, then, the road to western literacy contradicted the African oral tradition.

In this issue we invite you to listen to the voices of several South Africans and share their perceptions. The selections have been chosen as a sampling of the calibrations of color that make up the South African spectrum, without losing sight of the bigger picture that apartheid has always promoted the interests of White South Africans at the expense of others.

South Africans have turned to all aspects of culture to express their opposition to apartheid. Art, photography, theater, poetry, dance: All avenues have been employed, and some are easily accessible to the outside world. But we should never be so arrogant as to ignore the fact that many forms of expression are not conveniently translatable for a western audience, or even understandable outside of their cultural context.

Similarly, although this volume comprises contributions by South Africans of many racial groups, opposed to apartheid and sharing a vision of a nonracial future, it should be remembered that the volume also echoes the silence of those who have been disadvantaged, who cannot write, or who do not write in a manner or language that is understood in the western context, so different are their realities from our own.

For decades, apartheid South Africa with its discrimination written into law has epitomized racism. Now, after more than four decades of government-instituted inequality, brutality, and injustice, it has finally become clear to the government of South Africa that apartheid is unworkable, and it is being dismantled. However, even if all South Africans soon have equal rights, that will not erase the advantages that centuries of domination and privilege have given Whites. In addition, the dismantling of apartheid will not in itself answer the question of how to construct an egalitarian and ethnically diverse South

Africa. For South Africa, and for most democracies, equality will remain a burning question that goes beyond mere legality. All too often racism continues to survive under the glossy cover of equality.

Ethnic and cultural differences are here to stay, part of the diversity that preserves humanity from a boring and colorless homogeneity. Listening to the voice of the other, stepping into the other's shoes, seeing things through his or her eyes, as this issue invites you to do, is the first step across the bridge of difference that spans the raging torrent of "apart-hate."

Gary van Wyk, Consulting Editor

We are pleased to publish this volume of *Icarus*. We hope that our readers will discover in these pages a South Africa at once more complex in its self-identity and more familiar in its emotional landscape, a society in which the dignity of the human spirit has proven irrepressible.

Recognizing that the inequities of apartheid have affected South African literary expression, we have worked closely with representatives of democratic organizations in South Africa. We particularly wish to thank COSAW and COSATU for their invaluable assistance.

Patra McSharry, Commissioning Editor

Introduction

by Archbishop Desmond Tutu

The feelings of anticipation, euphoria, dread, and despair that have gripped the international community in the past two years have had remarkable parallels in South Africa.

In 1989 many of the characteristics of the Cold War era remained part of the international scene. Europe was still divided by an "Iron curtain" separating it into "East" and "West." Entrenched dictatorships and authoritarian governments seemed as firmly in place as ever. In South Africa, as recently as September 1989, police were beating people with whips and threatening them with tear gas for walking on beaches in protest against laws making it illegal for people of different colors to share the same stretches of sand.

By 1990 there had been a turnaround. Incredibly, the Berlin Wall had fallen. Regimes in power since the end of World War II were crumbling, and tyrants were being toppled everywhere. As the western media surveyed the end of the 1980s, they spoke of a new international order of harmony and peace coming to fruition in the 1990s. Early in 1990 we went through a similar time in South Africa. The South African government lifted the prohibitions on major Black political parties, it freed Nelson Mandela, and within three months the government and the African National Congress were sitting down for talks.

But then things went sour. Neither in the world nor in South Africa did the euphoria last. In the Soviet empire, conflict emerged, leading to repression that had overtones of the era everyone was predicting had passed. Out of that long-running sore, the Middle East, emerged the horrors of modern warfare, with great numbers of people being killed by weapons operated hundreds of miles away. At home, intercommunal strife in the South African

9

province of Natal reached new heights in 1990, and late in the year the carnage spread to the country's biggest metropolitan areas in the Transvaal. Negotiations began to bog down. The violence of elements of the security forces and the intolerance between political groups that has been spawned by apartheid threatened to derail the peace process.

In 1991 humankind stands painfully reminded of its vulnerability.

There is, however, another side to the story. That other side is found in the extraordinary enthusiasm of young people working for a better world, the commitment to the truth displayed by writers such as the contributors to this collection, and the resilience of human beings all over the world who face poverty, oppression, war, and racism.

I have had the privilege of seeing that resilience in many places: among Black people in Brazil, among those in African countries who suffer from starvation, civil war, and repressive government, among the Nicaraguans and the Palestinians. Traveling to these places, I have often wondered how I can minister effectively to people who are suffering so much. When I have arrived there, I have always found that they have ministered to me.

This collection gives us all the opportunity to experience the resilience of the men and women whose lives are depicted and to be inspired and ministered to by them.

MASIMBA!

NORMA KITSON

•Harare

ZIMBABWE

BOTSWANA

Messina•

MOZAMBIQUE

NAMIBIA

Transvaal

Nelspruit •

Mafeking•

⊙ Pretoria

Johannesburg •

Mbabane

SWAZILAND

Vryburg •

• Standerton

Golela•

Orange
Free State

Bethlehem •

Kimberley•

• Ladysmith

Bloemfontein •

⊙ Maseru

Natal

Richard's
Bay

LESOTHO

Cape

Durban •

• De Aar

Vanrhynsdorp •

• Calvinia

• Victoria West

Umtata •

Queenstown •

lantic
cean

• Cape Town

Port Elizabeth •

Indian
Ocean

Mosselbaai •

Norma Kitson was born in Durban, South Africa. She left school at the age of fourteen.

Ms. Kitson has received wide acclaim for her book *Where Sixpence Lives*, the story of her family's struggle against apartheid. Ms. Kitson was imprisoned and brutalized for her anti-apartheid activism, as was her husband, who was incarcerated for twenty years. Her book was named to the Kwanzaa Honors List and chosen by the *Sunday Times* of London as among the best paperbacks of 1987.

Ms. Kitson's articles have been published in the *Sunday Times*, *New Society*, and the *Daily News* of London. In addition, she has written a series of political articles for the *Labour Herald*.

Ms. Kitson has two children, Amandla Smith and Steven Kitson, and two grandchildren. She lives in Harare, Zimbabwe.

"*M*asimba!*" was written as a playlet and was first performed
by English actor Richard Seymour and the author's son,
Steven Kitson, on the picket outside South Africa House in
Trafalgar Square, London. It served to illuminate the political
situation in South Africa to the hundreds of demonstrators who
stood vigil day and night on the pavement from April 19, 1986,
until Nelson Mandela was released in February 1990. The vigil was
sponsored by the City of London Anti-Apartheid Group.
"Masimba!" was later performed by the author's daughter,
Amandla Smith, and Sheila Magadza at the Zimbabwe Women
Writers Public Reading in Harare.*

*Observing that the doublespeak rhetoric of the South African
regime seemed to fool some people, the author incorporated many of
the exact statements made by P. W. Botha, then prime minister of
South Africa, into "Masimba!" The piece has been updated from
time to time to reflect current political realities. Although F. W. de
Klerk is now prime minister, the author notes, little has changed in
South Africa, and the vast majority of South Africans continue to
live in poverty and under harsh repressive laws.*

You've probably heard tell of the day when the new
Prime Monster of South Africa visited the people at Stinkhole Bantustan. Because that was a historic occasion—
because of the honor of it. So I know you won't mind
hearing about it all over again.

A story is a strange thing that depends on the teller.
One person leaves the important bit to the end, another
puts it in the middle, and another leaves it out altogether.
The way this one was told to me, the bit about what
happened afterward was the important bit, and it got left
out. But, as I say, it depends on who is doing the telling.
And it also depends on who is doing the listening.

When you're sitting there on the bare veld of a bantustan with the cemetery behind you filling up fast, with the dust between your toes, empty stomach, no job, and the kids running around in rags, or naked, with big tummies and snotty noses, you aren't used to invitations to state occasions with important personalities. In fact, the most the people of Stinkhole ever got from a White official was a kick up the arse, a cuff on the neck, or the traditional greeting: "Bogger off, swartgat!"*

But now, now that the people have risen up, now that millions of people have been uprooted from their homes and thrown onto the bare veld, now that the money in South Africa's not so good, the Prime Monster was trying to sell the independence business and the negotiation business and a South Africa with no more apartheid, to the West—so the photographers had to snap him talking to the independent people, didn't they? Fraternizing with smiles and how d'ye-do's, as if we were used to eating ham and eggs for breakfast together every morning.

Of course, I wasn't there at the time. I'd have had to get special permission and a permit to enter Stinkhole Bantustan. And who'd want to go there, anyway? But I read an account of it in the newspapers and it sounded a very different story from that told me by a dapper young chap who was there that day. He was related to the bantustan chief, so he'd got himself a nice job and was working the system.

"It was like this," he told me. "It was a helluva great day for us. I am a clerk in the Administration. Nice job, man! Most people in Stinkhole got no money and got no job. I'm lucky, man! Most people got no water. I drink lemonade. But I'll never forget that day—Haai!

"The people came from miles around to hear the Prime

---

*swartgat—derogatory term for Black South Africans.

14

Monster. The Department of Works and Planning built a big wooden platform right there in the middle of a field. We shooed all the cows and demonstrators away. The mothers brought their babies, strapped on their backs. The old men came chewing their lips because there isn't nothing else to chew in Stinkhole. The old women came in their rags with their possessions in paper bags in case it was another removal. And of course all the cheeky Stinkhole youngsters came as well. Everybody wanted to see the big White chief—the Umkulubaas.

"There by the old gray tree, Chief Buthasebe was waiting in his finery to do the greeting. There was all the officials of Stinkhole baking in hot government clothes. And just when everyone was thinking, 'I wish I'd got money to buy a tin of water,' the big car arrived, and *there* was the Prime Monster. And there was me, I was there too, man—hot—in my posh wool suit, with a tie and everything."

"Forget about your tie and your suit, man," I said. "Get on with the story!"

"Hang on! Hang on, man!" says the clerk. "I have to mention the odd detail or two so you can get the picture. OK? It was a bladdy big occasion for us, don't you forget. There I was, opening car doors and escorting the VIPs around. I had a very important job, man! I was carrying files for this one, dodging blows from some of the White ou's,** and being careful to guide them all through the cow manure up to the platform. I was being very helpful, offering this one a compliment and that one advice. Hell, man! There was police on the perimeter and a lot of tanks—Saracens, Hippos. But we weren't expecting trouble, so nothing fancy. What a day, man! And there I was, one of the chief most important people.

---

*Umkulubaas—literally, "big boss."
** ou—person.

"They come to the platform, have a round of shaky-shaky hands for the benefit of the cameras, and I see the PM quietly get his hanky out and wipe off Buthasebe's shake. Immediately I whip out my Nat Party kerchief for him. He just ignores me. Whew! What a wonderful thing power is! It's very special, my handkerchief—orange, white, and blue for South Africa. It was a special line for the Tricameral Elections a few years ago. The Administration gave them to a bunch of kids in Stinkhole to wave around and sing 'Die Stem'—White national anthem, you know—but instead the buggers was dancing around and chanting: 'Be an Indian and join the mob! Be a Colored, maybe get a job! If you Black—get the Sack!' I went after them, I can tell you. But only with half my heart. I mean, who needs to vote, man! I've got my life greased up nicely. My wages gets paid, monthly on the dot. Put it in the bank, out comes the mortgage money—pop! Out comes the furniture standing order—zip! Out comes the little one's school fees—whoosh!—all automatic. And there's plenty left in the bank to buy burglar bars and self-defense items. Plenty left for me and the missus if you work for the Administration. Some people may not like it, but boy-o-boy just look at this suit, man—Savile Row, Germiston. And these shoes—Italian, made in Boksburg. And this tie! Everything of the best."

"Get on with it, man," I said.

"Well, first there's the whole business of shutting up the mob. Buthasebe even gets up and waves at them with his stick. At last the Prime Monster rises to the microphone. Now there's some silence, except for the SABC* cameras popping all the time. And he says:

"'I have come to Stinkhole to tell you people you've got your real independence. We not having apartheid anymore.'

---

*SABC—South African Broadcasting Corporation.

16

"The crowd went mad, man, waving and screaming: 'Masimba! Masimba!'

"The PM turns to us on the platform, he's so surprised at the terrific welcome he's getting: 'Hell, man,' he says, 'I didn't know you people are so enthusiastic about me. Man, this is the best reception I ever got in my life—here in Stinkhole. Where's those bladdy pressmen, hey? Mrs. Thatcher wants to see a photo of this so she can screw up the Commonwealth Conference and their bladdy sanctions business.'

"The security boer gives the photographers a few warnings with his sjambok* to get them going.

"Then the PM turns back to the mike and continues: 'You still getting low wages and you still not living with us, but we have outgrown the outdated colonial system of paternalism. In 1912 we had to grab all your land because we didn't have enough. Anyway, living on it, growing food, and keeping healthy like you was doing isn't what profit is all about, is it! And any case we civilized you all, isn't it? We taught you to suffer, like the good Lord says. We brought you measles, TB, VD, starvation, and lots of other things to save your souls.'

"'Since 1948 we Nats have been fatherly to you people, but *now*, now, because the bladdy Rand's gone to boot and the country's become downright ungovernable, we decided you grown up now. From now on you don't have to carry passes.'

"'Masimba! Masimba!' everybody yelled. Man, I only said, 'Bugger me!' when he said that. But that security boer gave me such a bladdy kick! Right up my new suit. No one could of even heard me. Any case he went on:

"'Now that millions of you people have been removed from the cities and there's no jobs, we repealing the pass laws. Instead of passbooks you going to have identity

---

* sjambok—a heavy leather whip.

17

books, OK? But you not living with us Whites, OK?'

"And the audience went crazy, man, waving and jumping about: 'Masimba! Masimba!'

"The Prime Monster was getting used to all the shouting by now and he waved them still. 'I see,' he continued, 'some left-wing newspapers have been having polls to see who's in favor of Nelson Mandela. I was sad to see 86 percent of you kaffirs (and some bloody misguided White traitors) said you were. That Mandela, he's an agitator. He's been giving us trouble for over forty years. And his wife too. I'm a humanitarian, Christian, God-fearing man, but when the women start getting into politics, you really have your hands full. Look at this Winnie, this Urbania Mothopeng, this Albertina Sisulu, Adelaide Tambo, this Marion Sparg, this Theresa Ramashamula, setting a bad example to all the women. Are they there in the kitchen cooking the meal for their husbands, their fathers and sons? No, they there bothering in the trade unions, bothering in the townships, bothering here in Stinkhole. Now I want to tell you, when the women start greasing your axles, man, it's the end of civilization—you just ask my wife. When we get them back in the kitchen, life's gonna be OK again.'

"And the cameras all went click, click. And the crowd yelled and screamed: 'Masimba!'

"The cameras caught him with his arms up, arms down, leaning back, leaning forward, mouth open, eyes up—oh, every which way. And eventually they started getting tired holding up those big videos and mikes in the heat. So the Prime Monster began to wind it up.

" 'We done a lot for you people. What you want all these trade unions for anyway? We just had to detain all the leaders and try to get things back in line again. After all, we done fine without trade unions for years, and our balance of trade was just terrific.

" 'And why d'you people want to live in shantytowns

when you can starve just as well here in the country! And we don't need the students, with their boycotts and actions either! Those students in Duduza and Kwathema, Fort Hare, Orlando High, in Mamelodi, Alexandra High, Vlakfontein—agitators! People agitating in Craddock, Lamontville, Umlazi, Vosloorus, Soweto, Langa, Natal, Cape, Transvaal, and OFS.

"'We cleared you people out of the cities into the townships, then to the bantustans and from there into the jails. We want a united South Africa where everyone loves each other in pure joy. If only the world would just give us a chance. We've got this State of Emergency going to help all this. We got a big army (even if half the buggers don't want to fight—bloody war-resisting agitators). We got guns and tear gas and even a nuclear bomb to win over you people.'

"The crowd went absolutely mad, man. He's a real orator, that guy. 'Masimba! Masimba!' they screamed.

"The Bishop was supposed to be there to end the whole thing with a prayer. But he never came to Stinkhole that day. So when the Prime Monster ends his business, he decides to do the praying himself. He downs his head, and there's silence. Suddenly Freedom, that young demonstrator, jumps on the platform, grabs the mike and shouts:

"'This evil which art in South Africa
Apartheid be thy name
Profit be thy game
Our will be done
You'll face our gun
In Pretoria
As you will in the bantustans.
For ours is the future
The power and the freedom.
So watch out, you boere—Bang! Bang!'

19

"There was a bit of a disarray. The security boer grabs the mike from Freedom, knocks him over, and gives it back to the Prime Monster. The PM screams upward to the kops on the perimeter: 'You bloody verdompte* lazy kops up there, come and get this bugger quick! It's another bladdy agitator!'"

"What happened after that?" I asked.

"They all went home hungry and thirsty. The cars drove off. Works and Planning zaps the wooden platform away quick before it's nicked. End of spectacle. End of story. Out of my hot suit. A lo-ong drink of lemonade."

And that's what I meant when I said it depends how it's told and where the important bit is and whether it gets left out altogether. Because a couple of days later, I got one of the pressmen to play me back the tape of that meeting. It was a bit blurred at the end because they were leaving the platform to go back to the cars. But as they went down the stairs I heard the bigwig Buthasebe say:

"Excuse me, Prime Monster, do be careful, sir. The cows have been walking past here. Don't step in the masimba."

---

* verdompte—Afrikaans term loosely meaning "bloody."

Insimba Isulela Ngemgqumshela

Obed Majozi

Obed Majozi was born to a farming family in Mthwalume near the southern coast of South Africa. At the age of 12 he left school to work as a gardener to help support his family. Two years later he was able to return to school. Upon completing high school, Mr. Majozi began working at a textile mill. In his seven years there, he became a union leader and organized union activity.

Mr. Majozi is a writer and poet. He lives with his wife, Gloria, in Durban.

*T*he impact of community vigilantes—or Mabangalala—*was particularly strong in South African townships in the early to mid-1980s. In general, the community vigilantes were older people or younger people with a conservative orientation who took it upon themselves to execute what they viewed as justice. Following the Soweto student uprisings of 1976, a generational split had occurred between young South African Blacks and their elders. Increasingly, youths were willing to risk their lives opposing state and local authorities in an attempt to bring about equality in South Africa. Meanwhile, a majority of older Blacks were unwilling to challenge the apartheid system. In light of this friction between generations, the tradition of respect for elders also broke down. Community vigilantes punished youths who were viewed as rebellious and who were frequently anti-apartheid activists; at times this resulted in the death of the youths. The police were generally supportive of vigilantes because of their conservative influence on the Black community.*

On the whole, the generational split was political in nature, but the following story does not focus on this political aspect.

The title of the story literally means "the mistakes of those in power are always smeared on ordinary people."

Mbhekelwa was terrified when he heard a voice say, "Shoot him down!" as he tried to escape through the back door; and when another voice said, "No! Use a sjambok!"* he froze on the spot. Unfortunately he was a tall fellow who could not hide among the guava trees in the yard.

It was the infamous community vigilantes. They had been called by Mbhekelwa's mother, Mantenza Msomi, to discipline her son, who had become impossible to manage since his father's death. His eldest brother, Mdelwa, who could have disciplined him, had left to work in

---

* sjambok—heavy leather whip.

23

Johannesburg even before Mbhekelwa was born and had not been heard from since. The family had given up on him.

When Mbhekelwa saw the young vigilantes, he was terrified because he knew exactly what he had done. No longer was he full of bravado that if anybody dared touch him he would turn the township into the battlefield of iSandlwana.*

"Don't waste our time! Why do you threaten your mother simply because she could not buy you clothes? Where do you think she will get the money when you don't even want to get a temporary job?" asked the spokesman for the young vigilantes angrily. Mbhekelwa denied it vehemently because he saw that the youths were angry. Some of the neighbors had come out to witness the action. Others, especially those who did not approve of vigilantes did not bother to leave their houses. They felt that the young vigilantes were taking the law into their own hands, and they did not want to have to appear as witnesses if asked by the police.

"Hold on to Brenda!" said one of the youths. Mbhekelwa knew what that meant because he had witnessed it. It meant he had to hold on to a streetlight pole so that the youths could administer corporal punishment. "Twenty lashes!" said one of them, and the rest agreed. Mbhekelwa started crying even before the first blow. It didn't help. "Give me the sjambok!" said the one who had pronounced sentence. He administered five lashes expertly and passed the sjambok to someone else to deliver the next five lashes. "Please stop it now!" said Mantenza. "He'll never do it again." Parental love and concern had won over the need for punishment. She even forgot that she had always wished her children were as good as

---

*iSandlwana—The battle at which the Zulu Army decisively defeated the British Army in 1879, and a highpoint in Zulu military history.

her neighbor MaZungu's. But the vigilantes continued until they had administered twenty lashes. Then they admonished Mbhekelwa to respect his elders and to behave himself.

As that very moment a blue police car appeared. The lookouts for the vigilantes gave the signal: "Comrades, they are here!" and everybody simply disappeared. Even the old people vanished into their houses. Mbhekelwa also disappeared. In a short time the police were all over the place with guns drawn. It was clear that if they had laid their hands on Mbhekelwa he would never have been seen alive again. The police were a law unto themselves.

Translated by Xolani Zungu

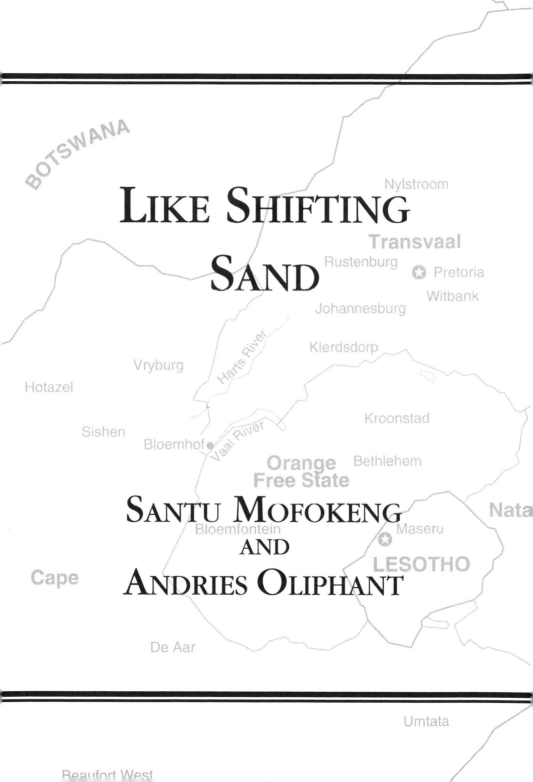

Like Shifting Sand

Santu Mofokeng
and
Andries Oliphant

Photo by Annemarie van Niekerk

Santu Mofokeng was born in Johannesburg and grew up in Soweto. Since 1988 he has been a documentary photographer at the African Studies Institute, University of Witwatersrand. In 1991 he was awarded the Ernest Cole Award for documentary photography. His photographs have been published in South Africa and abroad. The following photo essay is drawn from his first solo exhibition, "Like Shifting Sand."

Andries Walter Oliphant was born in Heidelberg, South Africa. He is an award-winning author, poet, and playwright who has written and edited a number of books, including *At the End of the Day*. His short stories have been published in several American, British, and South African publications, including *Contrast*, *Cutbank*, *Illuminations*, *Language and Style*, and the *Weekly Mail*.

He is currently editor of *Staffrider* magazine and general editor of publications for the Congress of South African Writers.

The flat, bleak, and drought-plagued plains of the south-western Transvaal, like most rural regions of South Africa, are home to White landowners and Black tenant laborers. This summer-grain producing region lies in the flood plains of the Harts River to the west and the Vaal River to the east and south. Red Kalahari sand and islands of limestone mark the arid topography of the region, which in almost every respect is a paradigm of labor relations in South African agriculture.

It was to this region that photographer and researcher Santu Mofokeng went for two years on assignment by the African Studies Research Institute. He was in search of the descendants of those who, in the words of Sol Plaatje,* awoke on a day in 1913 "to find themselves, not actually slaves, but pariahs in the land of their birth." On a farm named Vaalrand, in the vicinity of Bloemhof, a rural town on the Vaal River, the photographer probed the silent presence of the Black families ensnared in the tenant labor system and the agricultural cycle that constitutes the social and economic structure of their lives.

By befriending the community of laborers and integrating himself into the life of the Maine family—living and working on Vaalrand, the farm of Piet Labuschagne—Mofokeng came to experience and capture the texture of the farm laborers' lives. Home for Jakobus Maine, his wife, six grandchildren, and one great grandchild, he found, is a mud house with a leaky roof. The squalid interior he recognized as the starkly visible inventory of poverty. The evidence of psychological violence that registered on the faces of those denied the right to the land

---

*Black South African writer, author of the classic book *Native Life in South Africa before and since the European War and the Boer Rebellion.*

and reduced to being farmhands, moved him to reveal "the basic decency of marginalized and deprived people."

Working life for the Maines is ploughing and planting in spring, weeding in summer, and harvesting in winter. There are also cows to be herded and milked throughout the year. In spring and summer the sheep are sheared. Payment, on average, is 60 rand* a month plus a bag of mealies** when labor is in demand. Invariably rising at five in the morning and going to bed at about eight in the evening, they are caught in a pattern of repetition and variation, of change and nonchange, which is the code for the immobility, domination, and exploitation that pervade the lives of tenant laborers on Vaalrand.

Rest and recreation involve conversing, drinking home-brewed beer, and participating in occasional concerts. Life is basically framed, however, by labor and prayer. Mr. Maine prays in the morning, at midday, and at night. For him the omniscience and mercy of God are unshakable truths. In his company one is constantly reminded of Karl Marx's statement that "Religion is the sigh of the oppressed." Denied a full and just life on earth, Mr. Maine prays and hopes for a place in heaven.

On pension and payday the community comes alive. The grinding monotony momentarily gives way to the excitement of shopping. Staple groceries and small luxuries such as cigarettes and tinned food are bought from the local store, also owned by Labuschagne.

The children on Vaalrand are drawn into farm work until the age of nine, when they start school. School has two classrooms, a headmaster, and one assistant teacher. These two are responsible for teaching six classes. A paltry education designed for servitude and domestication

---

* At current exchange rate, approximately $24.
** mealies—cornmeal.

and lacking any incentive to learn yields dubious results for the students. Fourteen-year-old Mateatea Maine has, for instance, failed her first year at school four times.

In this world where the agricultural cycle is synchronized with the imperative of unrelenting labor exploitation, the silence cries out for change. At present, plans are under way to change the land laws that prohibit Blacks from owning land in the areas designated as White South Africa. At the same time Whites have been assured by the government, until recently, that they should not fear these changes since they are unlikely to forfeit any land. If changes are indeed in store in South Africa, the lives of farm laborers cannot pass in silence like shifting sand.

Andries Walter Oliphant

Limbless doll, Vaalrand Farm.

After the storm, Vaalrand Farm.

At the waterpump, Zevenfontein Farm.

Baby Fina Moss, seated, and her cousin Kebuweng Mokgali,
thirteen years old, Vaalrand Farm.

Sunflower harvest, Klippan Farm.

Family bedroom, Vaalrand Farm.

Jakobus Maine in his eighties, retired farm laborer, washing his face from a hubcap in the morning, Vaalrand Farm. His father and older brother were successful sharecroppers who came from Lesotho.

Koelie Moss surveying rain damage at Jakobus Maine's dwelling, Vaalrand Farm.

Pensioners on the way to paypoint, Vaalrand Farm. The bakkie,
or pick-up, belongs to Indian traders in Bloemhof.

THE PHONE CALL

HUGH LEWIN

Hugh Lewin is the son of British missionaries in South Africa. He attended Rhodes University in Grahamstown. After finishing his studies he worked as a teacher and a journalist.

In 1964, while working at a Black newspaper in Johannesburg, Lewin was detained and sentenced to seven years' imprisonment for his anti-apartheid activities. At the end of his term he left South Africa on a "Permanent Departure Permit." He moved to London, where he worked at *The Observer*, *The Guardian*, and *South* magazine. He moved to Zimbabwe in 1981 and in 1988 founded Baobab Books, of which he is publisher.

Mr. Lewin has written several books, including *Bandiet—Seven Years in a South African Prison*. He received the Parents' Choice award for his book *Jafta—The Wedding*.

Mr. Lewin lives in Harare, Zimbabwe, with his wife, Patricia. They have two children, Thandi and Tessa.

The Prison Regulations said No News. Politicals can have No News of Outside. They must not know what's happening Outside, they must not know of any political event Outside. They must be totally isolated. In the interests of the State and its Security.

The Politicals worked in the Carpentry Shop. This was a relatively small workshop accessible only from the inside yard and thus isolated completely from the outside, beyond the high wall round the yard, beyond the catwalk on top of the wall, guarded always by the man with a rifle. Inside the Carpentry Shop was space enough for four work-benches, each with its own tool cabinet, with a listed inventory of the tools in each cupboard. The list was checked at the beginning of each work session and at the end of each day to ensure that all tools stayed permanently inside the Carpentry Shop.

In the far corner of the Carpentry Shop was a door leading into a smaller room, which was the Office of the Carpentry Shop Officer. He was a large man with huge hands and a strangely pleasant smile, who checked the tools at the beginning of each session, and again at the end of each session, and then locked the tools safely away in their cabinets at the end of each working day. The rest of the time he spent in his Office in the inside corner of the workshop, studying his huge hands and cleaning his fingernails with a large penknife.

On some occasions he was seen to be sitting quite still, his chin resting on his fists, staring endlessly at the opposite wall. Once the unexpected arrival of another warder disturbed his apparent reveries and revealed that the Officer had, tucked into his hand, a very small radio that he was listening to—which, in a Carpentry Shop for Politicals, who had to be totally isolated, was strictly forbidden, even for the Officer. Sometimes he would

41

study the pages of a newspaper on his desk, quickly stuffing the pages into a drawer if any other warder visited the workshop. The prisoners, barred from news, were not allowed in his Office: They stood at the door, asking aimless questions while they stretched their necks to get an upside-down view of the news page, which was invariably long out-of-date or contained only sports news and comics, over which the Carpentry Officer would chuckle for long hours.

No great events rocked the inner sanctum of the Carpentry Shop nor disturbed its secure isolation from the rest of the prison and the rest of the world. But the Carpentry Officer did have, on the shining smoothness of the desktop in his inner office, one temptingly fascinating object of attention for the Politicals: a telephone. A telephone that worked, an aggravatingly tempting symbol of broken barriers, instant link with the great world of events and news outside.

The telephone didn't function much. It would occasionally ring to warn the Officer that some Important Visitors were about to descend on the workshop, whereupon he would scurry out of his Office to ensure that all was well, hustling and shining and busy in the Carpentry Shop. Sometimes the Carpentry Officer would appear to make internal calls, lifting the receiver and speaking to someone presumably within the prison because the call involved no dialing. Very occasionally he could be seen actually dialing a number himself: Then he would settle back into his chair with the receiver tucked under his chin into his shoulder, a contented look about him. On these occasions, he would often first lean across his desk and push the door of his Office so that it became partially closed to the inquisitive eyes (and ears) of the prisoners.

Every afternoon, having checked the tools in each of the tool cabinets and locked them, the Officer would return to his Office and methodically place a lock on the dial of his phone, then lock the key to the lock in a drawer, then carefully lock the door of his Office, then lock the door of the Carpentry Shop. Only once, the prisoners noted (for they watched these things), did the Officer forget to lock the dial of his phone before he locked his Office and locked the Shop, and on that occasion later in the evening, after lockup when the cells were all already sealed for the night and only just before the night man with his fiercesome dog appeared in the yard, the Officer was spotted hurrying back to the Carpentry Shop, presumably to fix the forgotten phone lock.

So, for the prisoners, ill-content in their isolation and perpetually seeking ways to bridge the walls of silence, the Officer's phone in the Office of the Carpentry Shop was thought of as an unlikely source of smuggled enlightenment. Greater potential seemed to lie in the chance that the Officer would one day bring to work more than just the comics and sports section of his newspaper, or that—a true prize—he would neglect to return to his pocket the mini-radio and that there would be some chance of lifting it. The telephone remained firmly in the realm of Outside, inconceivable as a part of Inside.

Until the day of the Big Visit. Nobody seemed to know *who* was coming, nor precisely when, but quite early one morning a young warder came running breathlessly into the Carpentry Shop and shouted that the prisoners had to line up IMMEDIATELY outside in the yard with their coats on and that the Officer must come now, *now*, NOW because the Chief was there and wanted to see him now-*now*-QUICK, and he shouted at the prisoners to Hurry-Hurry as he skidded out again and ran dementedly toward the Chief's office on the other side of the yard. The Carpentry Officer was, for once, considerably roused by this display of official energy and bustled around the prisoners as they downed tools ("Leave them where they are!") and fell into line outside the Carpentry door.

At first the Carpentry Officer stood firmly beside his line of prisoners, his bulky hands clasped behind his back and scowling for silence as everybody peered across the yard toward the Chief's Office, waiting for signs of the visitation. The young warder with the Urgent Message was hopping from foot to foot outside the Office, but there was no further sign of any cause for panic, and the Carpentry Officer, hands clasped still behind his back, began slowly to move across toward the Office, occasionally glancing behind him at the prisoners to ensure that they stayed silent and in line. By the time he reached the hopping youngster, the Carpentry man was all of 30 meters away from his office, able still to keep an eye on the line of prisoners standing outside it.

At which point the prisoner standing immediately in front of the door of the Carpentry Shop was able to slip out of line and back into the workshop itself, temporarily out of sight of the Officer and the other guards. Inside the shop the Officer's Office door stood open. The prisoner urgently whispered to his fellow prisoners nearest the door to knock loudly if someone returned from across the yard, then he nipped into the Office, going straight to the Officer's desk. There were only three drawers: The top one was locked and there were no keys in sight on top of the desk; the second drawer was open and cluttered with scraps of paper, but no newspaper; and the third had only an empty lunch box in it. No newspapers, no radio. Not even a morsel of contraband.

But on the shining top of the desk, sitting neatly next to a Prisons Department blotter full of doodles, was the telephone. The telephone, with no lock on the dial.

The prisoner quickly ran, bent double beneath the window line, back to the outer door and repeated the instruction to warn him with knocks if anybody should return. Then he scuttled back to the unguarded phone and sat down opposite it in the Officer's chair.

What to do? He was now four years into his sentence

and, after four years of isolation, he found suddenly he could remember no phone numbers. No, one: the number of his original home, at the village outside Pretoria, going back fifteen years: 65119. He could remember with absolute distinctness how his father, now ten years dead, used to lift the old black handset and say: "Hello, this is six five one one nine." Or his mother's more frequent "Six five double-one nine." But the rest, gone, blank. And the special dialing code between Pretoria and his hometown, Johannesburg, unused and unthought-of for the four years—gone.

It was madness. Here was a phone, unguarded, a godsend, but no numbers. The prisoner delved frantically back into the second drawer of the desk and found, among the papers, a tattered copy of a phone directory, for Pretoria only, without covers, but with lovely long lists of numbers. Whom to phone? Daytime, normal working hours of a weekday, and in Pretoria, where there had been so few friends. Whom to phone, and how to contact Johannesburg, where there were so many friends and wives of fellow inmates?

He found the name of a friend, a once quite close and sympathetic friend, but they had not been in touch for several years and certainly not during the trauma of the trial. Not sure even that he was still Business Manager at his father's firm. But here was the same name, and the telephone number of the firm.

Was that a knock? The prisoner jumped from the chair and ran to the Office door, but all still seemed calm, the warders standing in a chattering hustle across the yard.

Rush back to the desk but . . . how to get a line? Would the phone connect to the office across the yard or to a switchboard in the main section of the prison? Would they recognize that it wasn't the Carpentry Officer on the line? The prisoner lifted the receiver, holding it carefully, strangely, and coughed to clear his throat.

A woman's voice sounded: "Ja?"

He coughed again and said gruffly, thickening the accent as much as possible: "Lyn, asseblief. Line, please."

Silence. She said nothing. Had she suspected? He held on, his fingers straining on the handset, beginning to sweat. Then suddenly there was that old familiar click and the burr of a dialing tone. Just like that, Burrrrrrr. The prisoner laughed aloud, then hurried to find the number again in the directory. He dialed, dialed a simple telephone number again, so simple and automatic, after four years. It was ringing—again, the old sound, unchanged, almost welcoming—and another woman's voice answered, sounding younger, less guttural than the Prison's voice: "Knowles Brothers, hello."

The prisoner stuttered. "Is James there, please?"

"Mr. James?"

"Yes, please." Mr. James now, indeed. His hand still sweating, still no warning knocks from the outside door. And the less-guttural woman (What did she look like?) politely asked him—"Sir"—to wait. (Sir! Four years of abuse and being sworn at, and she called his voice Sir!)

"Mr. Knowles' office," said another, even sweeter voice. (What did SHE look like?) "Can I help you?"

"Is James Knowles there, please?" he stammered, unsure. Perhaps he was intruding.

"Who's calling, please, Sir?" So sweet, but some frigidity there.

"Tell him"—perhaps all the lines were tapped—"tell him it's an old friend, and it's urgent."

"Please hold on, Sir." Traces still of ice. Protective. But—"I'm putting you through now, Sir."

"Knowles here." The same voice, slightly high-pitched and with a touch of gruffness, yet instantly recognizable and slightly apprehensive. (Wonder if he's gone grayer?)

"Hello, James, it's me"—and the prisoner chuckled. He could almost feel the gulp and distant awkwardness from his friend. "Don't worry, James. It's only me and I'm still

Inside and I don't want anything. Just had the chance to phone and say hello." The prisoner, secure in his imprisoned isolation, comforted his Outside friend, surrounded by the complicated insecurities of freedom. "It's only me, James."

"Yes, yes. What do you want? I mean, how are you?"

The prisoner laughed again. "Sorry to bother you, and how are you? It's been a long time."

"Yes, yes, indeed,"—recovering—"but where ARE you? I hear you've had a rough time, yes?"

"No sweat. It's good to hear you. I'm Inside. But, please"—the sudden recollection of the Officer's Office and the line of fellow prisoners outside the door and the warders across the yard—"tell me what's been happening? Quickly, I've not much time. What's new?"

"Oh, nothing much really. We're all well. Oh, Dad died last year and I'm now in charge here, with Raymond. You remember? No, nothing's happening really, nothing . . . "

"James, quickly, what's the news? I've not seen a newspaper for four years. What's the NEWS, man, the news?"

"Oh dear, yes, well, I see what you mean. Hmm, yes, the news. Well, there's not really much happening, you know. Are you sure this is all right?"

"Yes, it's all right. But the news, James, what are today's headlines then, just the headlines? Read me the headlines."

But James couldn't find the morning paper, nor remember anything of importance from it, apart from a car crash, and the rugby team had lost.

"Internationally? The Sino-Soviet dispute? Middle East? America? Vietnam? Europe? What's been HAPPENING? What's happening in the townships? Anything happening HERE?"

"It's really rather difficult, you know. And such a surprise to hear your voice again, nice surprise. You sound so completely unchanged. Marvelous to think you're all right, well, getting through it all, all right, are you?"

"Yes, all right, James, thanks." The prisoner shrugged and tried to comfort his Outside friend: It didn't matter, really, and everything would be all right, but could he please look up a number in the Johannesburg directory, quickly please: the Stewarts in Parktown, Malcolm Stewart, probably somewhere like Houghton Drive, Parktown, if he remembered right. Yes, that sounded right, many thanks. And he scribbled the number on the back of a piece of sandpaper lying on the Officer's desk and— "Thanks, James, good-bye then. See you sometime"— putting the receiver back, clammy.

Outside the Office, the line of prisoners stood as before, watching the cluster of warders across the yard. No apparent change, and no sign yet of the impending visit.

So the prisoner ran back into the Office and, almost before getting to the Officer's chair again, lifted the receiver and confidently asked for "Lyn, asseblief" and, again, there it was. Burr-burr. The prisoner reached for the piece of sandpaper and then stopped: He had the Johannesburg number, but how to dial there? He had forgotten to ask James for the code. Was it perhaps 19? He paused, tried that, and got what could only have been an engaged sound. Slowly he replaced the receiver and wondered. Could he dare? Was there time? (Hurried check at the door—all well.)

So he tried again, easily now adding a greeting: "More, mevrou. Morning. Lyn, asseblief"—and again she gave him one and, with smiling care, he redialed the Pretoria number. "I've just been talking to Mr. James. Could I please speak to him again briefly? Thank you so much." And, straight through: "Hello again, James. No panic. Just what's the dialing code to Jo'burg? Thanks. Bye now."

Surely she would start to suspect something. Did the Officer ever make so many outside calls, so soon after each other? Maybe it was a big switchboard with several guttural ladies. Unlikely. What would she do, would she really care? What could they do, anyway? Worth the risk: "Nog 'n lyn, asseblief. Another line. please." This time she said nothing: burr, just like that. Easy. With extra care, the prisoner dialed first the code, then the new number, and it began to ring. This would be better, he thought: These friends were in fairly close touch with his family and knew his conditions, and were more interested in world events than James—and now he could ask the right sort of questions, quickly, straight away, feeling better prepared and more confident, less pent-up.

"Hello," said a strange voice, young but not Lydia's, and Colored-sounding. The maid perhaps.

"Mrs. Stewart, please," said the prisoner.

"Not here, master." Oh, my God—master. Their maid. Four years into a sentence for actions against apartheid and—MASTER. "Madam's not here, no, master. No, the master's not here either, master. Phone back this afternoon, please, master." Yes, all right, thank you—but how could he begin to explain the problems of trying to phone back this afternoon, any afternoon, and no, he's sorry he can't easily be reached if he left you the number, which he doesn't actually know because it's not written here on the Officer's phone? But, thank you, and are you well all the way over there in Johannesburg?

The Officer's phone . . . The prisoner suddenly realized there was something of a commotion outside the Office. He hurriedly replaced the receiver and just had time to reach the door of the Office when the urgent young warder burst through the line of prisoners and rushed into the empty workshop, his eyes wide, almost tearful, meeting the prisoner inside the workshop.

"Wat DOEN jy hier? What are you DOING here?"—it was more of a choked scream than a question and the warder at first ignored the prisoner and ran straight into the Officer's Office, looking around everywhere, pulling open the drawers and, finally, lifting the handset of the phone and staring at it.

"Were you here?" the warder shouted, still holding the handset and raging at the prisoner. "Were you HERE, I say!"—reaching again to a scream. The prisoner shrugged and stared back, gaining insolent confidence in the face of the young warder's hysterical discomfort. "Miskien, ja. Perhaps, yes." He turned his back and began walking out of the workshop. The warder stuttered after him: "Ek sal jou CHARGE. I'll charge you!" The prisoner looked back over his shoulder and shrugged again.

He was in time to slip back unnoticed into the line of prisoners just as the Commanding Officer and his deputy, with the Carpentry Officer and the several visiting dignitaries emerged into the yard and stepped formally toward them. It was an Official Visit from several Important People who, as they reached the Carpentry Shop, were greeted with a snappy salute from the young warder now standing alongside the line of political prisoners. The warder looked flustered but lifted his chin and shouted: "All's PRESENT and CORRECT, SIR!"

The Commanding Officer with the Carpentry Officer beside him nodded back contentedly, happy to see that the State's interests remained sound and secure, at all times. No chink in the armor.

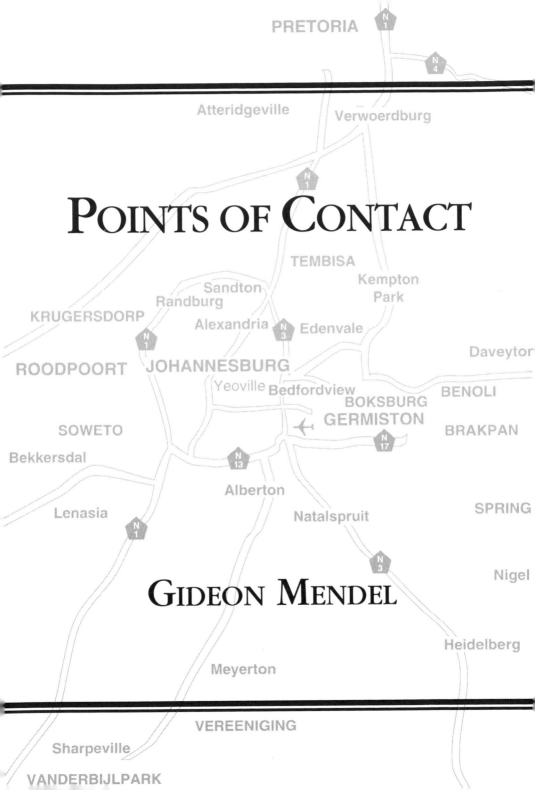

G ideon Mendel was born in Johannesburg. He attended the University of Cape Town, where he received a bachelor's degree in psychology and African economic history. He worked as a school teacher and as an assistant film editor.

Since 1984 he has been a professional photographer. In the course of his work he has explored diverse South African communities. His photography also took him to the front line of the conflict over apartheid. In the particularly violent period 1985-1986 he covered internal developments in South Africa extensively.

Mr. Mendel's photographs have been featured in *L'Express, Independent Magazine, Life, The Observer, Stern, Time*, and many other international publications. He has had a number of personal exhibitions at the Market Theatre in Johannesburg, including "A Broken Landscape," "Living in Yeoville," and "Promised Land." He was coeditor of *Beyond the Barricades: Popular Resistance in South Africa.*

Mr. Mendel currently lives in London with his wife, Yda Wilt.

Young people in South Africa today inherit a bitter historical legacy: centuries of colonialism, racial conflict, and segregation and the last forty years of apartheid, with its vast gamut of often bureaucratically implemented atrocities and the resulting social dislocation in which people of different races grow up experiencing vastly different worlds and perceptions.

Many Black youths face lives of squalor, with over-crowding, poverty, and inadequate education, whereas the majority of White youths have lives of relative privilege and comfort. The violence and conflict of recent years was an inevitable product of this configuration.

However, many Whites have been dissatisfied with the status quo and have joined the movements within South Africa fighting for an end to apartheid, and many Black people have been more than willing to accept Whites who genuinely believe in change.

The following pictures, taken between 1984 and 1990, explore the realities faced by young people in South Africa in numerous dimensions, from the horror to the hope.

Two boys at a public swimming pool in Yeoville, in central Johannesburg. The photograph was taken in 1987, when most public facilities were segregated. On this day the pool was closed to the public and open to children from various recreation centers. The recreation centers were also reserved for Whites; however, these boys were from a center in a "gray" area into which many Black people had moved in defiance of the Group Areas Act. The center had thus informally, and in defiance of regulations, become integrated. In the past year the Separate Amenities Act has been repealed, and public facilities are now open to all races, although in some conservative areas officials still attempt to bar Blacks from using them.

Black domestic workers care for White children at a park in Yeoville. Millions of Black women in South Africa are forced by poverty to leave their own children in rural areas to work for White families in the city. They often develop very intimate relationships with their young charges. The wages for domestic work are extremely low, in some areas as little as $30 per month.

New Year's Eve celebration in Hillbrow, a "gray" area in central Johannesburg. Over the past eight years thousands of Black people have defied the Group Areas Act by moving into Hillbrow, which is officially White. A densely populated inner-city area, it is now estimated to have a Black population of more than eighty thousand. Many of the newcomers have fled the overcrowding and severe housing shortages in the Black areas. They are, however, subject to exploitation by unscrupulous landlords in Hillbrow and to a lack of educational and other facilities.

A young boy whose father was shot to death by South African police is comforted at the funeral in Kagiso township, near Krugersdorp. His father was a bystander in a clash between township youths and police during a consumer boycott.

Youths in a township east of Johannesburg wait to ambush a police vehicle with stones. The violent clash began after police had fired on attendees at the funeral of a youth killed by police in an earlier confrontation at a funeral. Thousands of Black township residents died in this cycle of Black anger and police violence in the mid-eighties.

People of all races dance together at a "Bridge over Troubled Waters" concert held at a recreation area near Johannesburg in 1985, during a period of extreme political violence in South Africa.

A chess team from Soweto takes on the Yeoville Recreation Centre team in Johannesburg. The youth on the right is Watu Kobese, the South African junior chess champion. Regarded as a prodigy, he has defeated a visiting Argentinian grand master.

People of different races share a public shower on the Durban beachfront in 1987. At that point some beaches were newly integrated, side by side with beaches that were still for Whites only. In the past year, however, all beaches have been integrated as a result of a high-profile beach campaign of apartheid defiance.

Young migrant workers living at a male hostel in Soweto practice a Zulu dance in front of a patroling armored vehicle. The police patrol was part of "Operation Iron Fist," the state's controversial attempt to control the violence between Zulu migrant workers and township residents.

A dog protects a White household in Wendywood, a suburb close to Alexandra township in Johannesburg. The rising crime level in the suburb had induced an extremely high level of paranoia and security measures.

Children of White farmers on the northern border of South Africa carry their parents' weapons after target practice. The area had been subjected to numerous attacks by ANC insurgents.

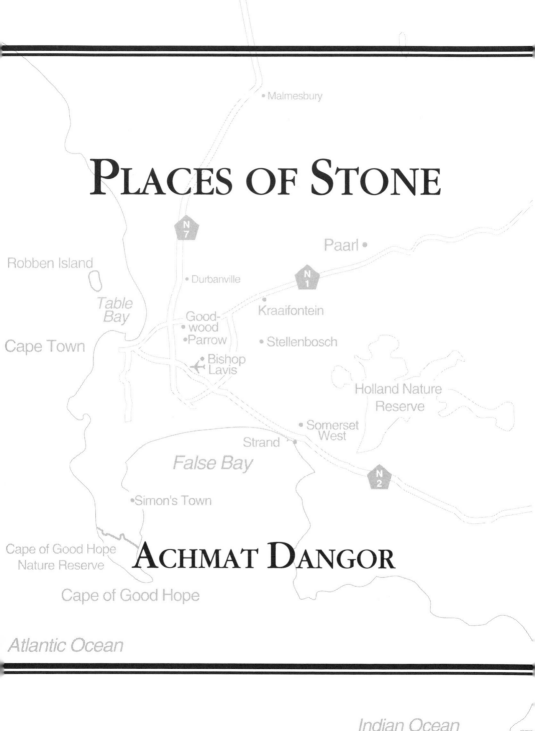

Places of Stone

Achmat Dangor

Achmat Dangor was born in Johannesburg. In 1970, during his first year at college, he was expelled because of his political activity. From 1973 to 1979, Mr. Dangor was banned by the South African government under the Internal Security Act. He is currently National Director of the Kagiso [Peace] Trust, a development organization that provides assistance to victims of apartheid.

Mr. Dangor is the author of *Waiting for Leila*, a novella for which he received the Mfolo-Plomer Prize; *Bulldozer*, a collection of poetry; *Majiet*, a play; and *2 Town Trilogy*, a novel. Mr. Dangor coedited *Voices Within*, which won the 1990 Book Award of the BBC Prize for African Poetry. In addition, his nonfiction articles have been published in Britain, South Africa, and the United States.

Mr. Dangor has two children, Justine and Zain. He lives in Johannesburg.

To Manuel this had always been a dark and somber land. When he had first arrived, many years ago, dark clouds spilled over the Mountain, and a storm was gathering in the bay. He was much younger then, a mere boy, and his body had been numb to the touch of the chains that manacled his hands and feet.

Now he felt the chains more acutely. It was a dark day, full of gathering storms, even though they were on the other side of the Mountain, far away from the bay of storms. The clouds were a black and silent mass, unbroken by the Mountain that caused the clouds to cascade over its rim and into the bay and the city. It was the silent heaviness of the sky, here, that depressed him most of all.

Manuel's owner was being buried.

Lying bitch! How the dead can lie. How futile, impossible it is to try to bring them to account for their lies. You only frustrate yourself, drive yourself into a state of impotent fury. Better to control yourself, accept that she had no way of keeping her word now.

She had promised Manuel his freedom upon her death. Now they were lowering her into the ground, and already his new master, the old woman's nephew, stood waiting to assume mastery over Manuel.

Johan Khul had inherited the old woman's property. He stood in a raincape and wore the scuffed boots of a Freeburger,* waiting to claim his property.

There was the house, with its gently sloping roof, built in the lee of the surrounding hills so that the powerful wind passed harmlessly overhead. The farm Mijne Rust, which means "my rest," the sheep, the two slow and unproductive cows, the young ewes and the ram recently

---

*Freeburger—free citizen, as opposed to a slave.

bought because the old woman wanted, foolishly for this area, to keep goats as well. And of course, the two slaves, Katie and Manuel.

Nowhere in her testament did it state that her two slaves were to be bequeathed their freedom upon her death. The old woman had not known much about such things. In any case she could not read nor write, and a landrost* had written her last testament. What did he care about the rights of manumission that slaves had?

To shorten his journey, the dominie had read the document at Mijne Rust before the funeral proceeded to the hilltop where the sentimental old woman had asked to be buried. Manuel, of course, was not invited to attend the reading of his dead owner's last testament, but he understood that he was not to be freed when Khul announced, "I am your new master."

The dominie was saying the Lord's Prayer in Dutch, and it had started to rain softly. Manuel knew that it was the last and late rain of the season and would not last long.

But the other mourners were restless and anxious to get the ceremony done with. They helped Manuel to heap the earth back into the hole and close the grave. Then Manuel was chained and shackled again.

"He looks so sullen and angry," Khul said in justification to the dominie and the family from the neighboring farm.

But they did not bother themselves with such a trivial matter. The sky was dark, and they did not like the gloomy place between the hills where this strange old woman had established her home.

They greeted Khul and his family—"Ask if you need anything"—and hastened on their way home.

Manuel struggled onto the back of the cart, hampered by his chains, while his new master waited patiently at the

---

*landrost—regional magistrate.

reins. Johan Khul's wife, a pale woman who narrowed her eyes shortsightedly whenever she looked closely at anything, sat beside Khul. And beside her their two children, who were about ten years of age and looked like twins.

The children had seen slaves before, disembarking from ships in the harbor, or at the Kompanje's* garrison, but never this close. And this was the first time that they had owned a slave. The children stared at Manuel and tried to touch him as a child would fondle a new pet. But Manuel's cold, grave eyes preempted that, as did a curt click of their mother's tongue.

Khul flicked the reins inexpertly, causing the horses and the cart to jerk forward.

"Slowly now, Johan, you've never driven a thing like this before," Khul's wife admonished him.

The horses settled down to a familiar rhythm of their own, leading Khul and his family to the house they now owned.

"Manuel. What a strange name for a Black man! Perhaps he's part Portuguese. Something gebasterd about him," Manuel heard Khul's wife say to her husband.

Khul did not answer, concentrating instead on trying to direct the horses that led them, with jerks and jumps, along a worn, uneven path that the animals evidently knew well.

He would get Manuel to even out the path tomorrow.

Manuel knew that this was not his real name. He remembered vaguely that he came from a place less mountainous, a place with flat fields where rice grew and people waded knee-deep in water. There was a great river, slow and brown with mud, but heavy with water that poured with crashing grace into the sea. He had had another

---

*Kompanje—The Dutch East India Company, which founded the Cape of Good Hope colony in 1652.

69

name then but could not remember it now. He was registered in the Slave Register as "Manual of Bengal."

Since the dim recollection of his arrival in the bay filled with storms and the darkness of clouds, Manuel's history had been anonymous. He was sold from master to master until he was brought to Mijne Rust by the old woman, who was already old then and who had lost her husband many years before.

Now there was this man with a carpenter's face who had never owned a slave and felt ill at ease with horses. May the sonovabitch die as well!

Manuel was glad that the old woman had resisted the temptation to till the ground, which was uneven and stony. She was content to farm with sheep and to keep the two cows that moved slowly and flicked their tails as they grazed, as if aware that their mistress demanded no more than enough milk for her and her household.

She was happy to let Manuel roam about the farm and mend things and perform his chores without rigid patterns or plans. She took charge only when the time came to barter their wool or mutton in the city or with neighboring farms for things that Mijne Rust did not produce. They rode in the cart, Manuel up front holding the reins while she sat stiffly beside him, her wrinkled face shaded by the dignity of her broad-brimmed hat, so unlike the bonnets that most women wore.

Johan Khul preferred to manage things himself. His first act was to sell Katie. "We do not need a house slave. There never was a need in the city, why should we need one now?" His wife accepted the burden her husband was imposing upon her with resignation.

"We mustn't allow this to soften us," she reasoned silently.

Manuel was alone in the cowshed that he had shared with Katie. This did not bother him very much. They had long ago stopped sleeping with each other. Still, it had been pleasant at night to feel another presence besides the slow, imponderable cows that chewed endlessly. The place where Katie had kept her meager belongings created a temporary void that Manuel had no time to ponder over, for Khul was changing things constantly.

Johan Khul wanted to grow things.

"What good is a farm where nothing is cultivated, where everything grows wild? A real boer* creates an order around him, makes things grow, gives them a pattern."

He made Manuel clear a patch of ground close to the house, in the same kind of lee that the house enjoyed.

"The first real rains will wash everything away. It comes off the hill fast, like a river," Manuel said, making a gesture with his arms that indicated a flood.

Khul ignored him and turned away, leaving Manuel with the bitter task of doing something that he felt in his heart was going to be futile.

At first the small heads of cabbage and other vegetables gleamed in rows above the ground, nourished by the natural moisture in the earth. Khul was triumphant, but reserved. He would teach his slave not only how to farm like a real boer, but some dignity as well. Working on a farm for many years—as a slave—does not make you a farmer. There has to be some greater plan to it.

When the sheep crashed into the vegetable garden and began to nibble the green, succulent heads of cabbage, Khul glared angrily at Manuel as if ready to strike him but did not do so. Probably because he had never struck anyone, not even a slave, before. The cultivated area was fenced off to keep the sheep and goats away. Khul also sold the two fat, languid cows and, combining the proceeds of their sale with the profit he had made from

---

*boer—"farmer" in Dutch and in Afrikaans.

selling Katie, purchased a real milk cow from the market in the city.

Toward the end of summer Mijne Rust had acquired an aura of well-being. The Khul family grew their own vegetables, produced their own milk and cheese. Manuel the slave was silent and obedient, having adjusted himself to the willful ways of his new master. Khul felt the need to celebrate. Over Easter he invited his family from the city to visit.

They came, mostly his wife's family, in a cart that shook and exhausted them, pulled by a team of asses that had the curious habit of stopping when anyone whistled. Manuel first heard them, the cries of one of the women echoing through the hills: "Moenie fluit nie, moenie fluit nie. Don't whistle!"

The visiting party bathed and rested and, as it was Good Friday, held a service on the stoep of the house, all of them seated in rows upon rough wooden chairs. Then the feast began. They roasted a whole sheep, one of Khul's elder relatives toiling before a huge fire that hissed from the drippings of fat. Manuel sat upon a rock and watched, joined by the dog that lay at his feet, red tongue hanging from its mouth.

It was peaceful sitting in the shade of the huge old tree, observing people making merry according to their custom. Until Manuel was summoned to help in the kitchen to wash things and clean after Khul's guests had eaten. His hands had grown used to working with rough things, with sheep and goats, and to using tools and moving rocks.

He broke things, not out of spite but because of inexperience. He had never been a house slave, and he became sullen at the scoldings he received. The Khuls and their guests regarded the recalcitrant slave as "part of the lot we have to bear." Part of the need to bring Christianity and civilization to this dark land. It became part of the prayers they said and the hymns they sang.

When at last, late into the darkness after Good Friday, the festivities ended, Manuel was able to go and sleep. In the cowshed Manuel found an elderly white man asleep upon the rough reed bed that Katie used to occupy, close to the nose of the new milk-cow, which regarded the intruder with large, indifferent eyes.

"Where's the meid that the old woman used to keep here?" he murmured to Manuel, then fell asleep again.

Manuel pretended to be asleep when the man, red-faced from the fire and the brandy that he had consumed, was fetched.

"Oom, dis mos nie menslik om so hier te kom slaap nie. Tussen slawe en kooie!" he heard Khul scold his uncle for sleeping among cows and slaves.

"Ek't net n' stuk slaafbout kom soek. Jy't die vekeerde slaaf ve' koop. You've sold the wrong slave," Khul's uncle replied in the bastard Dutch spoken by slaves and people of color in the city. He had come seeking to sleep with the slave woman, the drunken old man admitted candidly.

"We do not tolerate such un-Christian behavior here," Khul answered formally in Dutch.

Khul's voice was tired and irritable as he led his uncle back to the house.

A long while after the Easter period, with all his guests gone, Khul was still counting the costs in the number of sheep slaughtered and the depletion of the winter larder. Then it began to rain. Khul heard the sound of rain early in the morning, a soft, surging sound. The cleverly designed house did not take the full impact of the storm frontally.

This was the first significant rain that Khul had experienced since his arrival; it sounded soothing and rewarding as it washed off the roof. God had endowed them with something truly rich.

Khul dressed hastily and was still fastening his raincape when he stepped out onto the fresh, wet earth. The hillside had been transformed into a torrent of muddy water that poured into the fields with such crushing grace that Khul stopped and stared in awe at its beauty.

The vegetable garden was washed away, as was the track that he had ordered Manuel to build up with sand and stone. Khul looked fearfully toward the kraals where the animals were kept, but they had been constructed on higher ground and were safe. Through the veil of rain he saw Manuel in the roofed kraal where the milk-cow slept. The slave's face was calm and expressionless, but Khul saw in it a cold triumph.

Swine!

He felt a hatred for Manuel that would have enabled him to strike the slave mercilessly. But he went indoors, the cold rain too forbidding an obstacle for the moment, and sipped the coffee that his wife offered. It was too dark for her to see the tears streaming down her husband's face, mingling bitterly with the strong, unsweetened brew that he was drinking.

When the rain had stopped he found Manuel already at work, shoring up the areas around the kraals and the house with rocks and plaster made from cow dung and stone.

"What are you doing?"

"That storm was like the one we had so many years ago," Manuel said, raising four fingers of his hand.

"So?"

"It rained a lot. The water rose and flooded the kraals. And the front stoep."

Khul watched as Manuel resumed his work. It was the expression of sullen righteousness on the slave's face that bothered Khul, and the impertinence of his skill, and the authority it gave him over his master.

"You will do what I tell you."

Manuel stopped working and stood back from the half-built floodwall, his hands behind his back. Khul looked at the hillside, where the torrent had subsided into a steady stream, now clear and icily clean. Khul cursed the storm and the way it had betrayed him to this slave.

"Toe.* Finish what you were doing," Khul said curtly and walked back to the house.

It rained heavily that winter, so that at times even Manuel's floodwalls seemed threatened. Khul watched as Manuel sat in the kraal, seemingly indifferent to the danger, or was it that the slave's experience enabled him to calculate when the water would become a real threat?

Khul's anxiety grew when he discovered that they had been cut off from the city and from the neighboring farms. The ravines and paths that gave them access to the outside world, and escape from the fortress-like valley where their house stood, had been flooded, transformed into strong, surging rivers.

Manuel continued to milk the cow and bring the pail of frothy white liquid to the house. Khul's wife baked milkbread in the stove, and they ate sparingly of the cured meat from the larder. But Khul knew that if the rain did not let up they would soon not have enough to eat. Except the milk. And then they would have to begin slaughtering the sheep, or the goats, many of them just about ready to breed.

Khul cursed himself for the extravagant gesture he had made over Easter. As the rains continued he reduced their rations even further. Manuel, and the dog, fared worst of all.

Khul saw the solemn anger in the slave's eyes as Khul's

---

* toe—"get on with it" in Afrikaans.

wife gave the slave his evening meal. He saw Manuel empty his plate, the food untouched, into the dog's bowl and walk away into the rain. He heard the dog hungrily eat the food that Khul would gladly have given to his own family.

He became ashamed of the futility of his rage, at the way he snapped at his children, and because his wife recognized this futility. I will fix him in the morning! Khul vowed.

In the morning Manuel brought no milk, nor was the box of wood replenished. Khul donned his boots and went out into the icy, driving rain, forgetting to put on his raincape. His face was cold and pinched when he entered the dark and damp kraal, where he found Manuel seated by the cow, rubbing a sharp-smelling substance onto the cow's teats.

"What the hell are you doing?"

"She has inflammation."

"What from?"

"I don't know. Maybe all the damp hay she had to eat. Or we've been milking her too much."

"How do I know you are not doing this deliberately? Poisoning her or something?"

Manuel looked up at Khul without answering. His dark eyes were saying that Khul did not know, one way or the other.

For the first time in his life Khul raised his arm and struck the slave across the face.

"Get up. Let me see."

Manuel rose and allowed Khul to seat himself. The effect of the blow, which caused Khul's hand to sting, did not show upon the slave's face. It was as if he had absorbed the pain into a hidden, inscrutable area of his being.

The cow's teats were red and swollen. Perhaps that is how a cow's teats are supposed to look.

"How long will she be this way?"

Manuel shrugged.

"A day, maybe two. Maybe a week."

"What will we use for bread? It is all that is sustaining the children."

"Take the milk from the goat."

"The goat has milk? Why did you not tell me?"

"She feeds the kid."

"If we take the milk?"

"The kid will die. Too young to eat anything else."

Khul saw the tiny glint in Manuel's eye. He is making me choose between feeding the kid, which we need to start the goat herd, and feeding my children. The bastard is taunting me.

"Bring the goat's milk for the children. If the kid gets too weak we'll slaughter it for food."

"Your choice."

"Why did you not bring dry wood for the fire?"

"There is no dry wood. It has been raining for days on end."

"You should have thought of that before the rainy season started."

Again Manuel was silent, and Khul read in the man's eyes the question the man may have asked:

"You are the master, why didn't you think of it?"

The rain stopped and the cow got well, but it was too late to save the goat's kid, which Manuel slaughtered. Khul offered the skin to his wife. She touched the moist inside, as if the kid still snuggled there, then said quietly:

"You'd better dry and cure the skin. It will smell before long."

He was about to tell her to instruct Manuel to do it, he knew how; then he took the skin out of her limp hands. He would tell Manuel himself. Khul watched as Manuel went about his work, an unhurried, placid pace. The slave was nearing sixty, but his weariness was not physical. It was the solemn patience of the slave, the indifferent manner in which he obeyed the instructions given to him that bothered Khul.

And now Manuel waited for Khul to instruct him in all that he did. He no longer worked on his own and would wait for Khul to direct him rather than take the initiative in things that he had taught Khul about. Johan Khul was no longer free to walk quietly amid the green vegetation and observe the rows of plants, the simple pattern they formed but that nevertheless demonstrated the presence of human will.

He had to pay attention to all the minute details on the farm that he had normally left to Manuel; ensure that the cow was led out to pasture and returned at night to the kraal. Although Manuel did the work physically, Khul found it exhausting and exasperating constantly to walk about the farm and ensure that all the chores were done.

What good was a slave if he did not free the master from the daily, mundane tasks that needed to be done? Khul had ambitious plans for Mijne Rust, but he needed time to think and develop his vision. Manuel was not helping him at all, and he resolved to rid himself of his slave.

Despite his wife's opposition, Khul sold Manuel, described in the marketplace as an "experienced, well-trained slave. Very adept at animal husbandry," for fifty rix dollars.* The purchaser was Jool Baartman, the owner of a farm neighboring Mijne Rust. Baartman struck a hard bargain, refusing to pay more than one third of the market value of such a slave. No one sells a slave if he is all that useful, Baartman reasoned. The slave was probably a troublesome bastard.

Now Khul had to do all the chores himself. He rose early to milk the cow, feeling a strange peace within the

---

* rix dollar—a unit of currency introduced by the Dutch during their colonization of the Cape.

cool darkness of the kraal. He paused in his work to watch the place slowly being lit up by the morning sun. Next he drove the sheep out to pasture, using a cattle whip that cracked in the air instead of the stick that Manuel had used. Khul also did not make the strange, ridiculous noises with his tongue that Manuel did; he merely shouted "Hier! Hier! Back! Back!" to drive strays back on course.

The dog was useless at herding sheep and merely followed Khul around, stooping to sniff around in the deeper grass, searching for little animals that took refuge in the foliage. It infuriated Khul that, upon discovering a rabbit or squirrel, the dog would yelp playfully at the animal, totally without earnestness. The dog never gave chase to the "quarry"; it was a dog without any of the natural instincts of its kind, and Khul detested it.

He chased the dog away, lunging at it with his boot, before entering the vegetable garden to weed and water the young heads of cabbage. He looked sorrowfully at the tender, dried-up flesh of the tomatoes where the birds had pecked and resolved to construct a scarecrow. The curious scepticism of his city mind told him that birds were not fooled by such inanimate imitations of humans, but he would build one anyway. What else could he do?

Khul established a routine that was demanding and took its toll on his unpracticed body, for although the garden had been moved to higher ground and was now safe from flooding, weeds and wild grass sprouted more easily and needed constant attention. His arms were strong, but his back ached from the constant bending and scraping he had to do.

By midday Khul felt hot and thirsty and drank water from the well, using only his cupped hands. The water tasted sweet and was more refreshing than any water he had drunk. He sat down on the edge of the stoep and dusted his boots, surprised at how worn they were.

But Khul was happy, almost content.

He spoke Dutch to his wife now that Manuel was no longer around. He had a great distaste, in any case, for this pidgin mixture of a language that people were beginning to use, especially here, in places far away from the city. We have to learn to preserve our culture, our language, he often preached in his young, strident way.

"I suppose that these boots were not made for farming."

His wife's skin had turned a deep red and was beginning to darken from the sun so that her blonde hair hung in limp, glistening wisps on her forehead. She too had to share the burden of running the farm, caring for the chickens, cleaning their run.

"Johan, sometimes I think we two were not made for farming."

"Ag, nonsense. We'll manage. There's nothing a slave can do that we can't."

"Fifty rix dollars was very little for a male slave. Especially like Manuel, he was well trained."

"He was old, almost sixty."

"We could have obtained more if we were not so hasty. Enough to buy a younger slave. Help around the house."

Khul was silent. The tiredness in his body was like a void that had swallowed all the pressure he had felt before. The need to control Manuel, to give orders and make decisions, was a terrible, unrelenting responsibility. He was happy inside himself and determined not to let his wife's uncertainty infect him.

He rose and said quietly:

"I have work to do."

Khul began to learn about the hidden corners of the farm. The ravines where stray sheep fell and died. He learned how to salvage the flesh if the carcass was discovered before it began to rot. In the beginning he had to throw half of the flesh away because it had not been properly cleaned before being salted.

It was a struggle, but gradually he began to accept the drudgery. At the end of the day there was a peacefulness in the dusk that enabled him to forget the things he had left undone. He sat on the stoep and sipped the dark brandy his visitors from the city had left behind. Small compensation for all that they had consumed. Soon he forgot about them as well and thought less and less about the city.

There was silence all around him, apart from the gentle surge of the wind above the slope of the roof. The light from the lamps in the house lit up the surrounding darkness, providing a man-made refuge from the wilderness that surrounded them. It was as if Khul were at the center of the world and the source of its light and life. He was filled with deep and quiet pride.

Only his wife, tired from the many chores she had to perform both in the house and on the farm, brought a weariness to the serene atmosphere. She did not complain, but her exhaustion and her resentment showed in her eyes. At night when he went to bed she responded to his touch with a listless dutifulness.

The summer was coming to an end and Khul worked until late now, repairing the roof of the woodshed where the dry wood was stored. He would not make the same mistake again. It was dark, and he could see only the shadows created by the shape of the kraal and the shed and the dark hulk of the hills.

There was a rider at the edge of the rim of hills. Both man and horse stood in absolute stillness. Not even the mane of the horse, which Khul imagined would have flowed in the air because of the wind, was seen stirring. Khul hurried home, but both rider and horse had disappeared before he reached the refuge of his lamp-lit house.

From the elevation of the stoep Khul looked out into the

darkness of the hills, shielding his eyes with his hands as if from an extremely bright light.

"Did you see him too?" he asked his wife. "Manuel. The slave, he was there, on horseback."

His wife busied herself with the dinner, without answering.

"Johan, you have shut the door. Can you open it for a while? It is extremely hot in here."

Khul went about the farm, filled with apprehension. His wife had told him that his obsession with this slave—that useless old man—was ungodly.

"Everything you do is on account of the slave. You work on the farm alone, killing yourself, and perhaps us, because you want to prove something to that slave. Johan, he is just another pathetic Black that they caught in the jungle somewhere and brought here in chains!"

But Khul was certain that the rider he had seen was Manuel. The patient stoop of his shoulders, and his head gravely bowed like some wise elder. Yes, it was Manuel. The insolence of the slave was beyond belief! Khul searched the hills at dusk, slowly walking into the darkness, the old elephant gun loaded and cocked.

He saw the figure twice and on the second occasion was able to get off a shot in the direction of the rider. The gun went off with a booming recoil, sending birds in frantic flight from the thickets. The echo of the explosion rang for some moments in the hills, and Johan could see his family in the distance, watching anxiously from the stoep.

There was nothing at the spot where Khul thought he had seen the rider. The ball from the gun had shattered a tree, stripping the bark from the wood like skin ripped from human bone.

The next day Khul rode his horse, saddled and without the cart, to the neighboring farm. Because of his inexperience with horses, he sat hunched in the saddle, his knees uncomfortably high. He allowed the horse to trudge along the landmarks learned during previous journeys in the company of Manuel. He reached his neighbor's farm after a journey that took most of the day.

Khul stretched his cramped limbs and greeted his neighbor with excessive gruffness caused by the nervousness he felt. He was uncertain of himself and how his neighbor would react to his complaints about the slave that Khul himself had only recently sold to the man. Also, addressing another white man in this bastard language made him feel ill at ease, but he knew it was the language that Jool Baartman, strangely enough, preferred. He was in fact almost passionate about it.

The house was no different from Khul's house at Mijne Rust. Dark and angular, and cool in the stone-floored kitchen while the heat near the well of the grass roof was filled with the murmur of insects.

Baartman was much older than Khul and had lived on this plateau beyond the mountain for many years. He spoke in a sonorous tone, his language so inflected with words used mostly by slaves and Hottentots that to Khul he sounded astonishingly like one of them. But Baartman's voice had a cold authority that even Khul lacked and that allowed him to get to the heart of matters very quickly and brutally. Manuel had that ability.

A dog, half-blind with age, his skin no longer able to glisten, lay on the cool floor of the kitchen where Baartman received his visitor.

"Out!" Baartman said curtly to the dog, which raised itself stiffly and limped outdoors. "He's old now. Was once a real good watchdog. Could smell them in the darkness, the Hotnots and slavethings."

Baartman progressed without interruption from one topic to the next, about the locust plague the year before, and how it could happen again. "The first sign of the pests up there in the hills and you warn us, hear?" He cautioned

Khul about the inadvisability of keeping sheep in this area.

"They destroy the veld. Nothing grows after they've been through the grass." He had told Khul's aunt the same thing.

"Strange old crow that. You couldn't give her any advice!"

And without waiting for Khul to respond, he broached the reason for Khul's visit.

"But you didn't ride your arse off to come and speak to me about your aunt's madness—and befok she was, believe me—it's about this blerry slave Manuelthing, no?"

And so the subject of the slave Manuel was discussed. In the veld where he worked herding Baartman's cattle— on horseback—Manuel was unaware of the visit of his former owner. Manuel had had no experience herding cattle but had grown accustomed very quickly to their slow and tedious but deceptive habits.

Baartman had warned him not to be taken in by their docility.

"There's a madness in them like there is in slaves. When that madness comes up and makes them run, then nothing will stop them. Especially not a slave that's asleep. So don't let me ever catch you asleep here!"

The herd raised gentle clouds of dust as it grazed. The dust hung in the air, hot and still, so that Manuel had to concentrate and strain his eyes in looking out for strays. He knew that it would soon be time for the herd to be driven into the kraal, before the sun was too low. It was hard to see straying cattle in the darkness, which came with bewildering suddenness here.

But Manuel would wait until Baartman came riding out from the house to give him instructions. Manuel had not changed his habit of refusing to do on his own the things that his master should instruct him to do. Although he had not once since his arrival here disobeyed an instruction, his passivity was recognized by Baartman as a form of rebellion.

Baartman, unlike Khul, had many years of experience with slaves and was ready to punish them at the slightest hint of rebelliousness. He had struck Manuel with his whip many times since the slave's arrival, but although Manuel had winced, he seemed immune from the pain, absorbing the blows, and his master's heightened anger, behind the mask of his smooth, placid expression.

Baartman's wife in particular disliked this slave, whose graying hair and silent eyes gave him an aura of solemn dignity. When he first arrived he stood back from the other slaves, many of whom gratuitously scrambled for the food Baartman's wife gave them. It was a cur-like fawning, intended to please and flatter the "Missus" in the hope that she would leave behind an extra ration.

She noticed that the slave preferred to go hungry. It was an apt punishment for his insolence. He would soon learn. However, it was the other slaves who changed their habits. They stood aside until Manuel had taken his share, scrupulously in accordance with what was available, and then quietly dished their own, their heads bowed in sheepish dignity when they passed her.

"He looks like he could have a lot of trouble in him," she told her husband.

Now out of the rapidly descending dusk Manuel saw Baartman riding toward him, a furious cloud of dust in his wake. Baartman was screaming even before he had brought his horse to a halt, snorting and sweating from the hard ride.

"Get the blerry beasts back to the kraal, look how dark it is already. You dumb bastard! Do I have to tell you the same thing everyday?"

Manuel gathered the herd and began to guide them home. Despite the bad light, the slave had an astonishing expertise. He was clever and capable, but so damned stubborn. Baartman knew that if the slave stayed here he would have to crush that rebelliousness; very often such passive stubbornness could only be killed with the slave.

The district landrost set up a temporary court on Baartman's stoep, where in the languid coolness of an oleander he and his scribe listened to the evidence that Khul and Baartman gave. The slave Manuel, manacled hand and foot, was made to squat in a corner of the stoep.

In accordance with Kompanje's rules and regulations, Baartman, legal owner of the slave Manuel of Bengal, testified that the slave was not ill treated and had not been physically punished beyond the stipulated regulations. Manuel was asked if he concurred with this statement but did not answer. He was silent, his face dull and blank.

Khul described in a petition how he had inherited the slave, who had become, without reason, sullen and insolent. Khul had to been forced to sell him, at great loss, because of the disharmony that the slave had created on the farm Mijne Rust. He had also caused great losses, including the temporary barrenness of a valuable milk-cow.

He described how he had seen Manuel observing the Khul household "with great menace," even forcing Khul to shoot at the intruder on one occasion. The slave had illegally, without permission, used his new owner's horse to journey to Mijne Rust. It was a full day's journey there and back; it could only have been with the intention of intimidating and harassing his former owner and his family.

Khul was prepared to repay Jool Baartman one half of the amount that Baartman had paid for the troublesome slave, and he petitioned the landrost to have Manuel imprisoned "in a secure place," so that the safety and well-being of the Khul family could be ensured.

Baartman was asked for his opinion.

"Lock the damn stubborn devil away!" Baartman

answered curtly. Manuel listened to the exchange of words, to the scribe saying that he could not record such language. It would not be recognized and could jeopardize the whole case against the slave; there was the cry of birds in the thickets, and in the fields beyond the row of trees the cattle heaved in slow, bovine unison, dulled by the heat.

It would soon be time to take them to the water, which they trod into with ungracious haste, muddying the clear pools. It was always surprising to Manuel how quickly the river seemed to recover its flow, how quickly the pools regained their clarity. This place had an ability—beyond him—to restore itself.

The sea before the sun rose was calm, with the wind raising only small swells of water, with crests of silver, as far as his eyes could see. Manuel had never been this close to the sea before, and he found it beautiful, at first, to watch the sun rise as if out of the seabed.

Manuel's term of banishment to Robben Island—for "being a threat to the lives of the Burghers, the property and peace of the colony"—still had three years to run. How bright the island had seemed, as the boat, manned by six oarsmen, sped through the water. Seated in the prow, Manuel had raised himself to peer over the edge of the boat, watching the sea calmly race toward them.

He found it difficult to maneuver his body because of the chains that bound his hands and feet. The rattling chains aroused the two guards from their early morning stupor, but neither paid much attention to what the slave was doing.

"It looks like that one wants to jump."

"Let him. We'll see how soon he drowns."

Their conversation was nonchalant, indifferent. They soon turned their attention to other matters.

"Look alive there!" they shouted to the oarsmen.

A storm was gathering in the bay, and the Mountain was hidden behind a cauldron of black, surging clouds. Manuel did not jump. The dark, stormy mainland from which he was departing stirred uneasy memories in him, and he sat down within the deep recess of the boat to contemplate the vague, dim memories that took him back to the point where this life had begun.

On Robben Island Manuel was put to work in the stone quarry where prisoners cut and shaped stone to build the fortress and to expand the prison. He learned with remarkable ease to cut stone and raise it into walls of dull, forbidding gray. So quickly did he perfect his skill, in fact, that he was given more and more intricate work to do. He carved the innumerable crests and coats of arms that adorned each completed section until the walls were decorated with chains of talismans.

He cut the grooves into which the windows and doors would be mounted; deep, straight, and sinuous grooves that reminded him of the gorged out muscle sinew of gigantic men. He even learned how to fix manacles of chain into the walls of the punishment cells where difficult and rebellious prisoners were held.

After one year—Manuel found it difficult to keep track of time, since he disliked cutting meaningless notches into the stone of his cell—his hands had hardened, and his eyes seemed to grow dull from constantly staring at the rough and gray granite.

Time was forgotten; it no longer held any forlorn hope, nor was its slow, meaningless passing a source of anguish. He, like the stone with which he worked, had reconciled himself to the slow ravages that time wreaks. He would die one day, or his term of banishment would be over and he would be returned to the mainland. The walls were invisible, but no less hard and tangible.

He slept with the great ease of physical exhaustion and awoke in the slate-blue hour before the sun was up, his thoughts ingrained like rough rock. He had succeeded in crushing the agony of his imprisonment into a stone prison of its own.

Manuel did not mix much with his fellow prisoners and did not even hunger after news from the mainland, brought mostly by new prisoners and the rough sailors who manned the monthly supply ship. Even those who were doomed to life imprisonment on Robben Island, who had no reason to be influenced by the slow unraveling of history on the mainland, went to extraordinary lengths to obtain news from the city.

There was a small group, isolated from the others, who saved some of their rations to bribe guards for old copies of the *Koerant* that the prison governor received. What does it help them to know? Manuel thought. It did not even occur to him as strange that this small group of slaves could actually read. Just an additional, unnecessary burden.

To occupy himself, Manuel used the skill he had acquired to sculpt little objects from stone and discarded granite bricks. Figurines of soldiers that the Kommandant found attractive enough to display in his office. Manuel also had an eye for detail. He made mental note of the contours of the supply ship that called at the island each month and began to sculpt a model.

Guards and prisoners alike were fascinated by the ship that Manuel began to fashion. He sculpted one half of the boat, complete in minute detail, before proceeding to the other half, so that the sculpture resembled a strange animal that seemed to emerge from a womb within itself. When the sculpture was complete it had a mast and cannons that protruded from the side of the ship.

The ship gleamed with the white rawness of marble, the figure of a woman carved on its prow. There flew a flag of rigid gray.

"A pity it will never sail," the Kommandant remarked idly.

Indeed. All that the ship lacked was the inner

dimension of air and buoyancy that would have allowed it to float. When Manuel had completed the carving of the ship of stone, he abandoned it, heavy and immobile, outside his cell. Soon the rain, and then the hot burning sun, began to dull the raw marble, until it was no different from the other stone edifices on the island: gray and somber and lifeless.

For a long while Manuel did not carve anything. In his leisure hours he sat staring at the sea, or he lay on his mat in the darkness when the weather became hostile. He seemed to recede into the stone of his cell, indifferent even to the Kommandant who came to see "what the slave was carving."

He stood up obediently when the Kommandant entered his cell but did not reply when asked, "Ag! Why have you given up the work? You were quite good at it."

The man before Manuel had long gray hair that fell to his shoulders, leaving a powdery residue from his bad scalp upon the collar of the black uniform. And eyes like Khul's that do not look you straight in the face. What does he think of me as a man? The Kommandant's manner became cold and authoritative, and Manuel lowered his eyes.

The polished boots were the symbol of the man's power. He could crush Manuel beneath them as if Manuel were some kind of vermin. He remembered the old woman on Mijne Rust who used to pounce upon the lice that crawled upon her skin occasionally, and the way she crushed frantic, writhing shells beneath the soles of her boots. There was always a look of satisfaction upon her face.

Now the Kommandant was gone, and Manuel was upon his knees, searching for vermin he imagined infested the reed mat upon which he slept. He had heard the Kommandant say, "With regret, we have to place another prisoner with you. The cells are full. Anyway, he is a bad sort; perhaps your influence can change him.''

A man named Paulus was brought to Manuel's cell. He carried his chains in his hands because they were too long and hampered him when he walked. His ear had recently been cut off—to identify him as a dangerous slave, for he had participated in a slave revolt; Manuel could see the conch of flesh where the surgeon had stemmed the bleeding and sealed the wound.

Paulus sat down with difficulty, dropping his burden of chains in a coiled and gleaming heap. He was asleep almost immediately but groaned with pain throughout the night. He slept hunched up, his knees drawn up to his chest like one used to sleeping in confined spaces. As a result he did not occupy much room within the cell, but Manuel still felt uneasy at being so close to another human being.

In the plateau beyond the Mountain, Manuel could choose where he wanted to sleep, in the warm hay, close to the warm smell of the animals. Of course, there was a time he and Katie had slept together, soon after Katie first arrived. She was a house slave and slept in the kitchen so that she could easily respond to her Mistress' needs. But their sleeping together was out of the mutual hunger of their bodies, which ended with Manuel freeing himself from the warmth of her body, inevitably, long before dawn.

It was a solitary act of freedom to walk out into the darkness, aware of the sun slowly beginning to rise, with a raw incandescence, behind the hills. The taste of sleep in his mouth, and the first drink of sweet water from the well. Manuel remembered the dog nuzzling his wet nose coolly against Manuel's leg as he washed.

During the lifetime of the Old Woman, Manuel had acquired a habit of solitariness that most slaves are incapable of. And that prepared him badly for imprisonment.

91

Paulus stirred amid his rattle of chains, and Manuel wrapped himself tightly in his blanket, determined to fall asleep.

He woke, unaccustomedly late, to the sounds of the guards unlocking the doors. Paulus was already awake, sitting with his knees drawn up under his chin. Manuel noticed that Paulus had a very dark complexion, a blackness caused by the sun and the elements. He was also very thin, and Manuel imagined that the man must once have been stocky and powerful.

Manuel left with the other prisoners to wash and eat and perform his work for the day. He returned that night to find Paulus, his chains removed, kneeling in prayer in the Muslim manner.

When Paulus had finished his prayer he said to Manuel, "My name is Ali, not Paulus. That is my slave name, the one they gave me." He indicated the guards, who could still be heard outside their cell.

Manuel nodded and unrolled his mat. He was soon fast asleep; not even Ali's presence in the cell could disrupt for very long the rhythm of life he had established in over two years on the island.

Ali had no particular skills and was assigned to hard labor, splitting rocks and assisting artisans such as Manuel. From the beginning he refused to respond to the name Paulus, even at the risk of severe punishment, and he soon compelled everyone to call him Ali. The guards called him "Swart-Ali," or Black-Ali, because of his dark, scorched skin.

He was also called "Maargat-Ali," which meant thin-arsed-Ali. Although the Kommandant had forbidden the guards to use the gruff mixed language that the slaves used, the guards found it difficult to communicate with their wards in original Dutch. In any case it was a language that they took to easily, for it described so precisely the things that they thought about.

Ali accepted the sharp, graphic jibes that the guards used to describe him with great humor. He was a man who laughed easily, and his manner set everybody at ease in his presence. He was even able to turn the menace of his severed ear into an object of comedy, listening with exaggerated attention to instructions by cupping his hand to the conch of the missing lobes.

But his eyes were alive, searching the sea and the horizon as if trying to decipher a secret path away from Robben Island. Manuel noticed this alertness in Ali, the tension beneath his jocular manner. Ali laughed and clowned while constantly taking meticulous note of the guard routine, the change of the watches, the tides and the wind.

Manuel saw in Ali the madness of an obsession. In the relative privacy of their cell there was not much conversation, even though they were forced to spend many hours together. Ali prayed all the time, rising and prostrating himself, his prayers silent but nevertheless fierce, for his eyes were shut with the intensity of someone trying to expel the physical world around him. It was, Manuel thought, not only this stone cell he was escaping from, it was from all physical things, from physicality itself.

Manuel tried to shut out of his own mind the private, intimate act that Ali performed, which filled him with foreboding.

Manuel very seldom prayed, even when he attended the compulsory church service held by the dominie from the mainland who came with the supply ship once each month. Manuel listened indifferently as the dominie, at the end of each service, ritually warned his captive congregation of the price of heathenism. Eternal damnation of their souls! Was there anyone present who deliberately wanted to shut himself out of the kingdom of heaven?

Upon the cross of stone that Manuel had carved from raw granite upon the instruction of the Kommandant, a distorted, agonized body of polished oak was affixed. The eyes of Christ were raised, in tortured hope, toward heaven. Would he damn Manuel's soul, that suffering man nailed like a slave onto stone, any more than Manuel's soul was already damned?

Ali had finished his prayer. The cell was silent, and Manuel could hear the sound of the sea in the distance. A southeasterly was blowing; soon it would turn the calm sea into walls of raging water. And the rain would follow, icy squalls that clawed at the gray walls of the prison and the garrison.

Manuel wrapped himself in his blanket, welcoming the coarseness of its touch. He felt safe here, within the high, rough walls of the prison. He wondered whether Khul, on Mijne Rust, was struggling against the wind, the rain cold and fierce in his face as he battled to secure the sheep in their pen?

"Ek se ou, how long do these storms last?" Ali asked in the peculiar, resonant voice that made him sound distant, unreal.

"A few hours. The wind carries it across the bay. It will strike the mainland in an hour or so," Manuel answered, struggling to maintain his slow subsidence into sleep.

"Jurre, its mos goes amok ne! Can you sail in this weather?"

"I'm not a sailor, but I think it would be stupid to try."

"Has any ou ever 'scaped from this place?"

"I don't know. Not in this weather he won't, anyway."

"Manuel, give me your ship?"

"What?"

"That klipskip you carved. Give it to a ou."

"It is made of stone. It can't go anywhere."

"If you have faith. As jy glo, my broer, you can sail even

in a stone ship. Faith moves stone, vra vi' my. But you must have faith, imaan!''

Manuel was almost asleep; the wind had carried the storm to Mijne Rust. Walls of water came crashing down upon the fields, the house. My mud walls won't hold all this water.

"Well, I have no use for it. Have it,'' Manuel murmured, and fell asleep, uneasy that the vengeance he was wreaking upon Khul in this dream was so violent, so final.

The next morning it appeared as if the storm had been fierce enough to wash away Manuel's ship of stone. He wandered about in the calm aftermath, past trees that had been uprooted, to the edge of the gray and placid sea. The storm was not strong enough to damage the fortress and the prison. Why had it chosen that dull, immobile vessel of rock?

Manuel was surprised at the apparent power of the storm but soon dismissed the loss of his carving. He had learned not to become attached to material objects. He remembered little of his conversation with Ali, his mind preoccupied by the vivid dream he had had about Mijne Rust. Khul had been sucked into the vortex of the storm, his frail arms and legs flailing about like a huge, misshapen bird.

Three nights after the storm Ali disappeared. The night was astonishingly clear for a winter's night, and the stars shone brightly against the blackness of the sky. Ali did not return to the cell; for a while Manuel lay awake, for he did not want to be disturbed once he had fallen asleep. Gulls flew overhead in noisy squadrons.

Manuel knew, at last, that Ali would not return. The man's madness—or faith—had taken him on a journey aboard a ship of stone, undoubtedly to his death in the deceptively calm sea. The next day the island was searched and the prisoners were questioned. The investigation was routine and superficial. The foolish slave had probably drowned at sea, for the crosscurrents were strong and the water was extremely cold.

Manuel returned to his solitary life and habits. He cleared the cell of Ali's meager belongings, not surprised that the runaway slave had taken nothing with him. The winter was nearing its end, and Manuel, uncharacteristically, had a feeling of contentment. He had only this summer to wait before his term of banishment was over.

One morning, long before it was time to rise, Manuel was roused and roughly hauled to the Kommandant's office. There he found the Kommandant in his night attire, a long flannel dress and a woollen cap. He looked strangely shorn without the white wig of office. Manuel has never before seen a man in a nightdress, not even Khul who had brought to Mijne Rust many strange city habits.

The Kommandant was weary but obviously angered enough that he could not allow the business that had forced him to bring Manuel before him to wait until daylight.

"Your cellmate Paulus—or Ali, as he proclaims himself, has been reported to be on the mainland, preaching to the slaves. He preaches the particular heathenism that so many of you eastern people are afflicted with, the faith of Mohammed. As a mark of that faith—he is reported to be saying—he escaped from this island on a ship of stone."

"Meester, no one can sail in a ship of stone."

"I know that. You must have helped him. Another boat perhaps, or you know a way through the currents. You're a clever fellow."

The inconsistent and incredible interrogation of the cowed slave continued until the Kommandant was weary and had seated himself on his throne-like chair beneath the window. The sun was rising, red like drenching blood against the winter sky.

Manuel was sentenced to another ten years of imprisonment on Robben Island "for complicity in helping a fellow prisoner to escape." He was assigned to hard labor, and the privilege of a single cell was removed. He was no longer allowed to keep his artisan's tools.

He was no longer able to fall asleep with the ease of peace and weariness. In the crowded cell in which he had been placed, men stirred and murmured and made the unprecarious noises of slaves in a cell. They farted loudly, and those who shared blankets with each other out of the years of loneliness did so with a stealth that was almost chaste.

Manuel remembered that he had not slept with a woman for many years, long before Katie was sold. And the Old Woman before Katie came. Does Khul know that secret? Ah, but why do I call her 'the Old Woman'? She was no older than me. It was loneliness and hunger. She used my body for sex the same way she used it to clean the kraal or herd the sheep. It was a measure of my slavery.

Yet how much that old woman despised me when she found out that I also slept with Katie.

Manuel did not hold anything against those men who slept with each other; it was one of the prices paid for being imprisoned here. It was the heat of that summer and the suffocating closeness of human bodies that kept him away from his fellow prisoners, isolated in the little corner he secured for himself.

The summer was a meaningless season now, one of many seasons of heat and mist and the dull glare of the bluegreen sea. Manuel used half of his already diminished rations—for one whole month—to buy a stone chisel from one of the artisans. In the corner of the cell he had claimed —and protected—with the gleam of reckless madness that showed in his eyes, he began to carve miniatures of the supply ship. They were simple and hastily produced carvings, without the love and patience that his previous carvings showed. The guards laughed at the crudity of these stone figures and ignored them.

But the story of Ali's escape had spread throughout the prison, fantastic tales of the slave aboard a ship of stone that cleaved through the heavy seas, driven by a wind that rose from the depths of the sky. Of Ali's faith that had conquered the walls of stone and overcome the forbidding, sinister ocean that had been up to now Robben Island's most impenetrable wall.

There was much excitement, especially among the Muslim prisoners. The Kommandant, purely as a precaution, ordered the guards to confiscate the miniature ships and to find Manuel's tools. The slave was to be put on punishment rations of bread and water. When that failed to stop the appearance of the small vessels, in all corners of the prison and even on one occasion on the beach itself, he ordered Manuel to be placed in the solitary punishment cells.

Still the Kommandant's informants among the slaves reported continuous mutterings among prisoners, especially the Muslims from Batavia and Java. One even said that they were preparing for a mass escape on ships that Manuel had carved and hidden all over the island.

Then, to everyone's astonishment, a larger ship, very much like the one that Ali was said to have escaped on, was found among rocks close to the sea. Slaves and common prisoners alike were in a state of excitement. The workforce became sullen and surly.

It was time—the Kommandant knew—to act. Manuel was brought before him, manacled hand and foot, vainly trying to shield his eyes, which had grown accustomed to the darkness of the punishment cell, from the glare of the sunlight.

The heat within the stone walls of the Kommandant's office was unbearable to the guards and the Kommandant, who, in defiance of the rigid dress code demanded of someone of his station, had unbuttoned his tunic completely. His chest was brawny and tattooed with the figure of a gigantic leaping fish. Probably a sailor once, or even a felon, who had redeemed himself through hard work, luck, and bribery.

He raised his gleaming boots onto the desk, the bloodstains of innumerable vermin on the soles. Now the Kommandant was on his feet, fanning himself furiously.

"I could have you shot for inciting the other prisoners. Or simply throw you into the sea. Who would know? No, do not speak," he said to Manuel, who showed no intention of attempting to speak. "I could brand you, cut your ear off to mark you as a dangerous animal, and return you to the mainland. You would be hunted wherever you go. Ah, but why make a martyr of you?"

Manuel realized that the Kommandant was really addressing himself, debating aloud what the fate of this troublemaking slave should be. What did Manuel know of martyrdom, or even what the word meant? It was foreign to his vocabulary.

"Slaves do not become martyrs," he heard the Kommandant say, "they die or live because their masters decide that. You will not become the martyr of Robben Island. Fortunately for you. Your master Johan Khul died during a storm recently. His widow petitioned for your return—you are her rightful property—to the farm Mijne Rust."

With a wave of his hand, the Kommandant dismissed Manuel.

Burdened again by the chains that bound him hand and foot, Manuel was escorted to the dock to await his turn to board the supply ship. He noticed that a storm was gathering in the bay.

Surely they would not set sail a such a storm? Suddenly Manuel became fearful of the journey ahead. Even if he survived the turbulent sea, what lay in store for him at

Mijne Rust? Another "old woman" bitter from being abandoned in a distant and inhospitable place where life offered nothing but continued struggle against the elements and against one's own loneliness?

He thought of Ali, the crazy logic of the man. "Even a chain can warm you, if you hug it to you like it was real sheepskin." Manuel began to think of all the warm places on Mijne Rust, the kraal at night amid the rustle of warm animals, the stone platform beside the well—heated by the midday sun, it was like a cocoon of heat even in the heart of winter.

Manuel seated himself on the floor of the wooden jetty, his fears slowly subsiding in a flood of memories of Mijne Rust. A slave's life was like a ship of stone. You had to have faith in it.

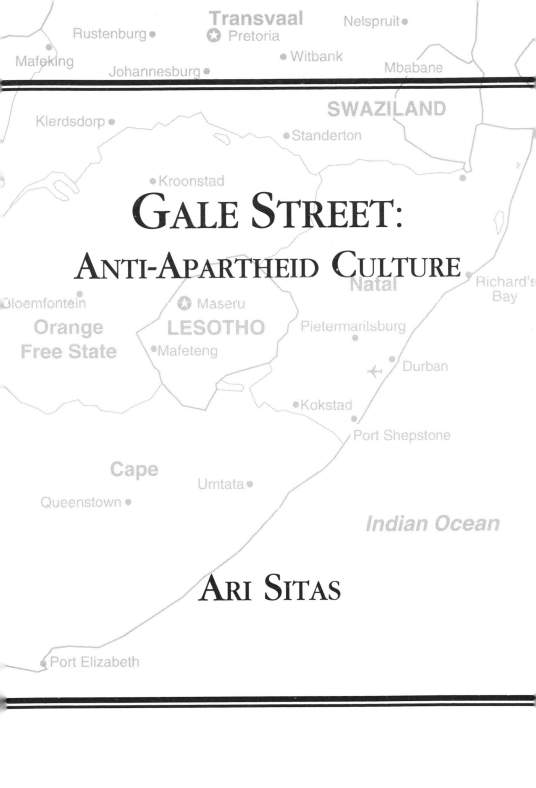

GALE STREET:
ANTI-APARTHEID CULTURE

ARI SITAS

Ari Sitas is a sociologist, writer, and poet. He is a founding member of the Junction Avenue Theatre Company in Johannesburg and since 1980 has been involved in trade union activities. He was an initiator of the worker theater movement in South Africa. Since 1983 he has worked with unions in the Durban area. Mr. Sitas was involved in the formation of the Durban Workers' Cultural Local and the Culture and Working Life Project. In 1987 he helped found the Congress of South African Writers, and he continues to serve as an executive member in the Natal Regional Office. His books include *Tropical Scars*, a collection of poetry.

Mr. Sitas now coordinates the Industrial and Labour Studies Center at Natal University and is an editor of the *South African Labour Bulletin*.

The photographs in this essay were contributed by South African photographers Chris Ledochowski, T. J. Lemon, Cedric Nunn, Paul Weinberg, and Gisele Wulfsohn.

The essay was a collective effort on the part of the writer and photographers and was coordinated by Paul Weinberg. It is itself an expression of the collaborative tradition that has developed out of the struggle for a united society in South Africa. Ari Sitas' text is one of eight stories that will be included in *The Irrepressible Struggles of a Workers' Cultural Union*.

For the last month I have been observing the slow demolition of "Gale Street." The demolition, that is, of the building in Durban that housed the trade unions on its ground floor and friends on its first and second; "Central Court" was its real name. For many, this rathole, with its dust, its bad ventilation and poor light, its grime and makeshift furniture, its half-torn posters, told the story of the growth and strength of our local trade union movement. For me in particular, a late arrival on this twisted coastline, it signified the growth of a cultural movement.

Beginning in 1983 we gathered on the ground floor, either in the MAWU* or the TGWU** offices, and tried to make plays. After the trade unionists had folded up their files and locked up their cabinets, and some, it is true, locked up the converted toilets they used as offices, we used the large rooms as rehearsal spaces: 3 × 3 meters, and if you bounced around too hard the dust would tear at your innards from your sinuses to your tissue. From the apartments above hung with their customary bare light bulbs you could hear funky music through the floorboards. You had to shout to whisper in a play.

Every late afternoon until 1986, Gale Street was the rehearsal space for trade union cultural work. All the historic decisions and ideas of the day would hang out in the rooms like stale tobacco smoke as we for our part would strut about as bosses and workers, lovers and victims, and so the Durban Workers' Cultural Local was born. Plays like "The Dunlop Play," like "Why, Lord?", like "Usuku" found their plots and narratives in those spaces. None of us knew that some of the sparks that were

---

*MAWU—Metal and Allied Workers' Union.
**TGWU—Transport and General Workers' Union.

being produced there would someday ignite a broader, more assertive resistance culture.

The DWCL, as the Local came to be known, consisted of a small core of people. So small that it wouldn't take the security police more than a single night to round them up. All of these people were resolute, committed (to various causes), talented, and too busy to have a personal life: They were activists of a special type! But it was also made up of dozens and dozens of migratory characters.

The latter variety would arrive, observe, demand, improvise, perform, and usually leave frustrated. Many saw the DWCL as a place of potential opportunity—a place to show your talents, your shoeshine, a place to captivate the nation, a place to earn a dollar and get rich. Others saw it as a place of militant resistance—to express your feelings, your aspirations, and to chant down apartheid, the capitalists, their friends-and-all. Of course, there were also the grassroots Romeos who heard about women dancing and playing: Dressed to kill, they would arrive swooning. The oral historian of tomorrow will discover the richer underlife that was the backdrop for the plays that poured into trade unions and political gatherings.

But what was in the mixture that was poured into such gatherings? That has aroused much scholarship and debate, so I must tread cautiously. (First I would like to apologize for starting sentences with a "but" or "and," our teachers always insisted that that was wrong. But . . . it has the same sense of rebellion against authority as saying things like "creating together" or "authoring your own life," of being more than a horde of numbers, productive units, and commas in someone else's script. And, as we found out, it was exciting to excite others.)

Nevertheless the talents and feelings that entered the Local cannot be understood unless a broader issue is tackled: the invisible thread that connects the countryside to the cities, the cities to compounds and hostels—in short, the migrant labor system and its apartheid strictures. And within that, the poverty of working class communities, the cheapness of Black labor and life, the appalling conditions: the infrastructure that allowed oral forms of communication and culture to survive, for survival purposes. To survive and cope, you sang, you danced, you composed; you defied, subtly.

There is also the need to understand the politics of sense, gesture, and smell: the texture of what was available to us before it gained confidence through political struggle. To understand the pain of the textile Black/woman/worker's monologue and the sexual innuendos of her dancing, you need to know about the collapse of the rural homestead, the alcohol that drowns its elders, the rudimentary flea-bitten, summer-sweated hostel room she tried to run from, her daily grind, her attempt to flee through sexual favors into a better township environment, and that the soft flesh around her midriff was from a pregnancy she didn't plan for.

Finally, yes, performance traditions, their languages and their accessibility to our audience was also necessary for our understanding. The power of oral forms of poetry, the constraints of ethnic dancing, the popular sense of presenting a story, the familiar vocabulary of church music and so on. All these were poured into Gale Street and into all the other Gale Streets all over South Africa, and these in turn shaped the way people speak of "struggle."

From 1984 onward, resistance-based performances occupied any and every public space made available by political and trade union organizations. And so the Local traveled.

In our travels we were staggered by the variety of and clashes in creative expression.

On day one you would be performing on modern paving stones, suffocated by the smell of fresh asphalt

Purple rain day, Greenmarket Square, Johannesburg. Policeman threatens to arrest musician for creating an illegal gathering. "Purple rain" refers to the spray police sometimes use for purposes of identifying participants.

The South African Communist Party launches in Soweto.

Birthday bash celebrating Nelson Mandela's 70th birthday at the UCT Great hall, stopped by police minutes later.

being laid out nearby, surrounded by people with hip T-shirts and jeans, mingling with traditionalists about to dance *ngoma*-style, egged on by their supporters in rural attire waving home-tailored hammer and sickle flags.

On day two you would be crammed into a hall draped with slogans and campaigns, with sweat and smoke, with rhetoric and speeches, a quick shuffle of furniture and there: On the platform stands Qabula, the worker poet from Natal who delivers his lines emphatically but much more slowly than in the agile days when he would frenetically shake the gathering. The poetry is slower, bleaker, harsher. Before the applause dies down, another performance stalks the platform. Speed up: comedy, humor, satire, the surreal realism of the underclasses tearing figures of authority to shreds.

On day three, at a workers' book launch: chanting,

ululating, and then the sonorous hostel choirs singing in the styles that made Ladysmith Black Mambazo famous: *isicathamyia, mbube.* After that the gospel choir, the *amakhwayia.* All of them immaculately dressed, spending their last cents buying the suits and ties to complement their choir, buying the white gloves and socks, the maroon and purple jackets. And there, putting their souls, their biostructures into their call-and-response croons. They would be followed by a youth group doing a *gumboot* or a *pantsula* dance, adorned with chants and slogans. Then those white anticonscription crazies would go on stage and mock the military.

Day four somebody would get shot, hacked, knifed.

Day five would see the crowds pouring into the streets for the funeral: Residents would place buckets of water and cloth outside their doors in case there was a tear gas attack. The youth would be out in their military uniforms, with their militaristic chants, their symbols of war. The endless toyi-toyi rhythms would slice the afternoon. Songs and chants whose lines speak of the spear of the nation, the AKA (AK-47) and bazookas.

Day six would take you to a union hall: There they are again, the Sarmcol Traveling Players. This admirable group of strikers from the Natal Midlands, who have been trying to win their reinstatement since 1985, have become a theatrical institution. Their plays, "The Long March" and "Bambatha's Children," have excited popular audiences for years. Their mixture of humor, song, dance, and struggle captivate everybody.

Day seven: roadblock. All the Local's subversives line up against cars. Evidence necessary to link this loose group of "agitators" to some cosmic plan engineered by none other than the, cringe, AFRICAN NATIONAL CONGRESS and its, cringe, allies to overthrow the government. The evidence is piled out in front of the car: guitars, microphone, good luck charms, leopard skin vest, a toy truck,

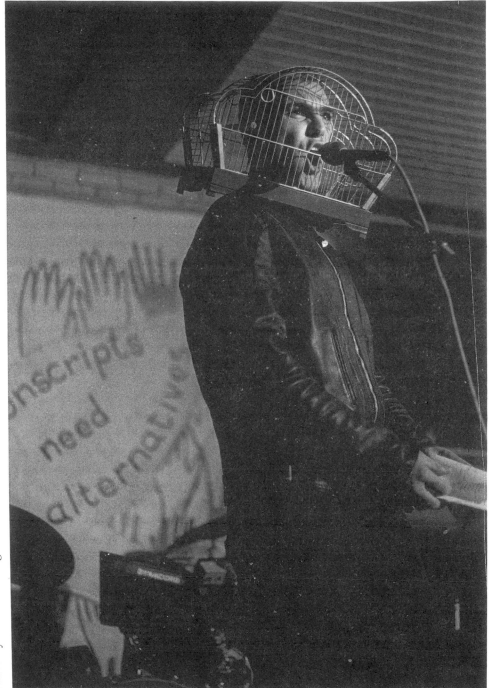

Matthew Krouse reads a poem at an End Conscription Campaign concert.

Photo by Cedric Nunn

Scene from ''Bambatha's Children,'' performed by the Sarmcol Traveling Players, workers from the Sarmcol Rubber Plant who went on strike and were fired.

Photo by T. J. Lemon

ANC supporters welcome the release of Nelson Mandela.

Trade union workers dance the toyi-toyi at a Congress of South African Trade Union Workers' congress.

school uniform, banner with slogans, cardboard, suspenders, trumpets, chair, necklace, headgear, flannel pants, traditional attire, peaked cap, little floral skirt, plates, noose, khaki pants, a cop cap, a toy pistol (wooden), a toy pistol (plastic), T-shirts, underarm deodorant. An irritating wait, in the end laughter all the way home.

Day eight: Bomb at COSATU* house.

I was convinced twice that we had to record the irrepressible history of this "cultural local," to preserve the stories and images that we confronted. The first time it happened out of pain and laughter. The pain first: We were asked to host a rehearsal of a Midlands play at Gale Street in order to empower ourselves, to learn about directing, and to help others with our experiences. We

---

*COSATU—Congress of South African Trade Unions.

111

Scene from "Death Penalty," performed by the History Work-shop, Witwatersrand University.

ANC supporters dance the toyi-toyi (a liberation dance), Eastern Cape.

agreed. But the facilitator of this magnificent undertaking was urgently required to sing in a project somebody else facilitated miles away in Johannesburg, and so on and so forth. We were faced with a group of workers, hot and bothered, complaining about Durban's humidity and an array of beautifully crafted masks. The masks were papier-mâché heads of cattle, large and poignant, large enough for mass gatherings and colorful enough for drab surroundings. But they had no slits through which to see— Aha, we intoned, for us to learn empathy, for us to feel our way next to each other. With initiative I led: I donned a cattle head and started demonstrating the perfect movements of the creature. And at one moment when I reached out to balance against a door I knew to have been there, the door opened and I went cruising past an amused trade unionist and into his converted-toilet office to lose a tooth

113

and blood against the protrusion where the toilet paper used to hang.

And laughter: After returning from the hospital I heard that the rehearsal had been canceled because of a police raid on the Gale Street unions. The policemen arrived to find a room of braying and neighing creatures walking around, bumping up against each other, and sporting beautifully crafted bovine heads. With the unionists and documents they took, the police also took photo studies of themselves with their freshly caught mooing game. According to reports, Brigadier Erasmus had never in his twenty-five years on the force experienced the likes of this. Not only had he posed again and again with his game in front of guffawing underlings, but he insisted that the group accompany him to headquarters to demonstrate their talents. Once inside, apart from the derision and mooing sounds, they were faced with blank sheets of paper: Write everything down, they were told. They didn't.

The second time I was convinced we had to write and preserve the little stories and images we collected from all over South Africa was when I walked out of the Gale Street fish and chip shop after a lengthy argument about vinegar on my chips, when I saw furniture piled outside Central Court. By then the unions had moved out. By then cultural activity sought more sophisticated venues. By the next week people with tape measures had arrived. And then the pounding started. Let words then speak for its walls and the dreams that were made there, and perhaps there will be found a few pictures so we can tell the children: The one there, half-naked dancing, was your mother . . . and . . . you see we flapped and also danced despite the choke.

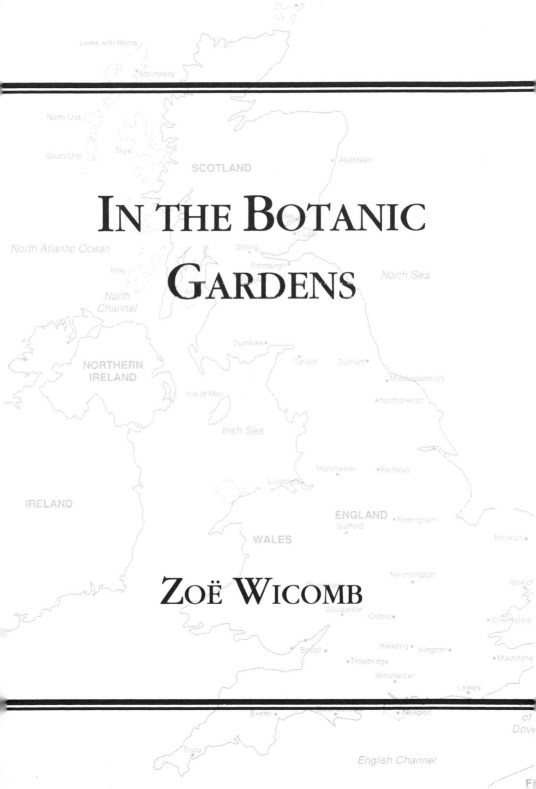

IN THE BOTANIC GARDENS

ZOË WICOMB

Zoë Wicomb was born in Cape Town. After spending many years in Britain, she returned to South Africa to teach English at the University of the Western Cape. Ms. Wicomb is the author of the highly acclaimed *You Can't Get Lost in Cape Town*, published by Pantheon. Her short stories have been published in a number of journals, as well as in the anthology *Colors of a New Day*.

Ms. Wicomb lives in Cape Town.

$\rm T$here were several accounts of his last movements. But she remembered only two. And the first only dimly, so that she imagined that it had been whispered by one of the other South African students, a girl called Tsiki, who held her hand and puffed continuous smoke into a small narrow room: He had been brought home by a friend who saw him to his room at 11:30 pm. Then he had disappeared.

The other was delivered by the man from the British Council, Mr. MacPherson. Dorothy Brink did not quite catch his name but decided that Sir would be an appropriate form of address. The man was in national dress; he wore a green tartan kilt, a short tweed jacket, and tassels on his socks. He spoke very fast so that it was difficult to follow him, but perhaps she would not have understood anyway. This English was very smart, she supposed, quite different even from the English of the SABC news reader; he might as well have been speaking a special language understood only by those in national costume.

She tried to concentrate but could not get rid of the funny feeling that these sounds did not add up to functional words that would tell her anything about her son. For she could summon up no image of Arthur, whose blue aerogrammes lay in a ribbon-tied bundle in her bag. Like a lover's letters. She knew them by heart; she had read them all night long. This soft, clipped voice claiming to follow footsteps now, twelve days later when not an echo remained, prevented her from imagining a young man called Arthur. She wanted to ask what shoes he wore, but here in Glasgow her English would squeak like crickets in a thorn bush; besides, the man did not expect her to say anything. He had introduced her to himself: "Eh, Mrs. Breenk" and replied to his own enquiry after her welfare, "How are you? As well as can be expected, eh?" Not that Dorothy was not grateful, for she seemed to to have control over the thickening of her tongue, but if she could hear something like "black brogues" perhaps then she could understand that he was indeed speaking of Arthur, a young man who stood with her only three months ago in Bata's in Kerkstraat and explained, "Mamma, they're back in fashion." But these kilted words were about inaudible footsteps in a strange city where she had as yet not seen a single person in black brogues.

They sat in a room that reminded her of the in-flight film that she saw through an insistent reel of still images. Of Arthur as a toddler, in his school uniform, with the first traces of a stubble, at the airport with a scholarship to Glasgow University. An elegant room, Michael Caine said from the corner of his mouth as he strode about, idly—and rudely if you asked her, she had certainly taught her children manners right from the start—picking up an ornament before sitting down in a chintz armchair. Then Arthur as a young man, never ashamed of helping her with the housework. She had waited by the door while her host emerged from behind his desk to shake her hand. They sat in a cluster of chintz chairs and coffee table at the far end of the room, and like Michael Caine she looked at the high ceiling while the man in the kilt poured coffee from a glass pot with a plunger. At the cornice, elaborately molded, and the ornate ceiling-rose, an intricate pattern of spiky leaves, and she recognized the paintbrush heads of flowering thistle. A room of muted colors in which to speak about a death. The walls were a pale gray, the woodwork a shade deeper, the plush carpet another bluish gray, and looking out through the tall windows, sets of panes imposed a grid on the vast canvas of uniform gray representing a sky that spoke nothing of the weather. For by weather she understood either rain or the clear sky of Namaqualand.

She started at his movement. He placed his right leg across the other, his left hand clutching the right ankle.

118

His eyes wandered, then came to settle just below Dorothy's left ear lobe. She dropped her eyes to the large knee, a brutally scrubbed plane of cartilage, and resolved to concentrate. He was still speaking of the Botanic Gardens where a guard saw a young man at 11 pm who answered to the description of Arthur and whom he recognized as someone who frequented the Kibble Palace. But why was he telling her about the huge hothouse? He had said that she should go and see the place for herself, and she had nodded dutifully. But he went on:

" . . . a lovely structure, our Kibble Palace—very old— built a long time ago on Loch Long, where it was privately owned, and then the entire glass structure was floated down the River Clyde on a raft. Brought to the Botanic Gardens in the nineteenth century. But it's unbearably hot, of course. Tropical conditions, you understand, for these marvelous plants from all over the world: Australia, South Africa, New Zealand, India, and, of course, America. Absolutely marvelous, like traveling . . . "

Arthur wanted to travel—right round the world. Wanted to be first an engine driver, then a pilot or a ship's captain, nothing special, just dream-boasted like the other children, like Jim and even little Evvie. A slight boy in short trousers and scarred knees, darker than the rest of his skin, almost black, who stuck his hands into his pockets and with the remarkable combination of lisping and rolling his r's that she knew would take him far, managed to say, "Sthee-e, sthee-e, when I come back with bagth full of money I'll marry Mamma and we'll have sthweeth every day."

She shut her eyes momentarily to wrench her mind from the image of the boy and concentrated on the man's words. But he too had slipped up, had allowed his mind to wander, so that he carried on like any tourist guide:

" . . . also the People's Palace is well worth visiting. Another glass structure, smaller, but devilishly hot too—

eh, for the plants, of course. Lovely tropical things. The rest of the building is a museum—the history of the working people of Glasgow. You'll find that interesting, coming from South Africa. Very important to have these records. Of the struggle . . . eh . . . you'll understand how here in Scotland . . . but remembering the people of the city, eh, that's what being human is all about. Aye, well worth a wee visit and not a bad place, of course, to have a bit of lunch either, eh . . . "

He faltered as Dorothy leaned forward, frowning. How could Arthur be the subject of this talk? What was the man saying? Who was this man in the kilt? She had surely come to the right place; he had expected her, welcomed her himself. Or was he speaking in code? Arthur had once said to her after a strange telephone conversation, Don't worry, you can't speak plainly anymore; you can't be safe without a code. Ag, then she let it ride; she didn't want to be bothered with such things now, now knowing nothing of politics, she was failing Arthur. A bird flapped its dark wings in her chest. Panic widened her eyes.

Mr. MacPherson, whose words had strayed so wantonly, bit into a syllable then shot out a hand that hovered in the horizontal to steady her. He had seen television images of South Africans at gatherings, Black women ululating and stamping their feet, and really he would not know what to do about such behavior in the office; he would steady her with practical advice.

"Mrs. Breenk, you'll need distraction of this kind. This is a difficult business, eh, coming to terms with Arthur's, eh, eh . . . but above all it is important to keep calm. The People's Palace is out with this area but trying to find your way is, of course, good for occupying the mind. Keep going and you'll keep in control."

As if she would lose control here among strange White people. Oh, she did not understand this talk that had nothing to do with her and it was all her fault, no good finding out about a code now when it was too late. She, a woman without learning, who had not managed to keep Arthur from politics, could only sit quietly and obey the hand stretched out like a dominie's with blue veins and liverish patches, commanding her to remain seated. Only when the hand dropped to his side and the knees moved and the body folded out into the vertical did she read his movements as a sign for her to rise. Her movements followed his; the navy blue handbag, held with both hands before her, faced his sporran apologetically.

"So, Mrs. Breenk, as you can see, we're doing our best. But," and he paused to look at her gravely, "one must be realistic. It would be foolish to hold out too much hope."

She did not care about her words squeaking. In a high voice that ran like mice along the curlicues of the cornice, she said, "Yes, sir. No hope. I have no hope at all. But it's the body. It's, please, the body, sir. I am his mother; I must see Arthur's body."

He pressed his hands together in pointed compassion. And lowered his voice.

"Mrs. Breenk. I understand. I understand your concern, but we are doing our best. We shall have to be patient, but I can assure you that the police are doing their best."

"Sir, I would like to speak to one of the other children from home. There was a girl, Tsiki; I saw her yesterday . . . "

"I'm afraid, Mrs. Breenk, that won't be possible. These young people—and not only the students from South Africa—have a heavy program. An unfortunate time really. You see, they're taking exams and we here at the British Council are concerned that the unfortunate disappearance of Arthur should not cause any further upset among our students. It's a difficult business being a student in a foreign country where you're not only contending with new ideas but also a foreign language, of course. I think you'll agree, Mrs. Breenk, that further contact with the other students would be inadvisable. Young people and especially the young women are so vulnerable, so easily upset."

Mr. MacPherson pried apart his hands for the greeting. She fumbled with the bag and transferred a scented handkerchief to her left hand in order that her right could be vigorously shaken by him.

A taxi waited to take her back to the hotel, and she had to say that she was well looked after. That at least she could take back to Vlaklaagte: that the British Council provided taxi drivers who said Yes Ma'am and drove her to a comfortable, if old-fashioned, hotel.

Also, a nice young woman from the British Council had taken her to the hotel last night even if she did go on rather foolishly about the light switches: on and off as if she were God trying out the sun on the first day. On. See. Pointing to the lamp shade suspended from a high-as-heaven ceiling, and Off, with a voice inflected for darkness. Quite ridiculous, and funny how it made her think of the oil lamps of the early days. Arthur was the one who could not bear a smudge of smoke on the lamp glass. He kept it sparkling; always particular, her Arthur who loved his Mamma, she promised herself, loved his Mamma, but the girl asked if she wanted to try for herself—On. Off. She shook her head. Whatever would these people say next. Still, it had been easy enough to understand the girl who said, as if she could read her thoughts, "If you prefer to eat alone here in your room, just telephone down and order something and don't worry about money. The British Council will see to everything." She wished she had asked Arthur what this British Council business was; she had hoped to ask one of the other students.

Dorothy eased herself onto the bed still holding the handbag, its base pressed against her bosom. Her cousin Celie's bag, for she had decided that she would not wear black, would not believe the worst. Navy blue crimplene was smart and, she sighed, a good compromise and she wanted everything to match, to ensure that Arthur would not feel ashamed of her. So particular he was—Always look your best, Mamma—with that fastidious flattening of lips against his teeth as he checked her clothes for the prize-giving at high school. Her boy who did not want to know about his father, about the fathers of Jim and Evvie—men whom she remembered only as eerie, elongated shadows that fell now and again, accidentally, across the frowning or smiling faces of her children. She had barely begun her story, choked with shame, when he interrupted, "Mamma, it's just you and us and let's not talk about it, let's not talk about anyone else. You've done everything by yourself. From nothing you started the shop and look now everything's OK. That's all I want to know." Or something like that, something that promised to wash away the shame of twenty years and from Arthur, her youngest, who was so particular. Too particular? That's what Celie thought, she knew what Celie-them thought, but no one would dare say anything to her.

From the start, from the very moment of his conception, there had been a weight in her womb that told of the specialness she was carrying so that she hardly registered the disappearance of the man. Or perhaps she had just come to expect it. But this time she didn't care. The fetus absorbed what little shock there was. She loved the child who lurched about wildly in her belly, a child who wanted to be born. No ambiguous flutterings in the womb; he moved purposefully and three weeks before he was due maneuvered into position and fought his way out, a strong, healthy baby. If surprisingly slight.

No ordinary boy he; she knew that he would be a bank manager or a president or something even bigger, although she warned him against messing about with politics. Always particular he was, her Arthur. How, and Dorothy's fists beat at the pillows, how could they tell her that there was no trace of him, that he had just disappeared? Just a name? A missing person? An absence? A nothing? Oh, she felt the emptiness, the lightness that would make her body rise to that heaven-high ceiling and cackle at the nothingness that had been her soul snuffling against a handbag.

She grabbed the handbag, slipped on her shoes and coat, and rushed out. She would not cry here in this barbarous place where no one cared to find his body. That was what the girl, Tsiki, had said. That they had done nothing: A tired police constable had arrived two days later to ask obscure questions and did not come back. That it was a conspiracy, but she did not know what that could mean.

She would find her child and she boldly hailed a taxi, one that stood right outside the door as if it were waiting for her, to take her to the Botanic Gardens. The man did not say Ma'am; he asked her for money and shrugged and shook his head and just held out his hand when she said British Council. He joked about her twenty-pound note— Lots of money, eh—and gave her as change a ten-pound note with a picture of what seemed to be smiling Africans. Something was written across the image in blue ballpoint pen. This man was not to be trusted. To hell with blarry mysteries and secret codes. Politics was one thing but joke currency quite another. For ten years she had been running her own village shop successfully; a businesswoman was not to be fooled in this way.

"Listen man, here in England the notes say Bank of England," she said, and in response to his frown added, "No good sitting there with a mouthful of teeth; if you've got something to tell me why don't you speak? I'm a shopkeeper. I trade groceries for cash; don't think you can cheat me with signs and codes," and checking the other side of the note, "and false money from some Clydesdale Bank."

The man engaged a gear as he hissed, "Bank of England! Where the hell do you think you are? This isn't bloody England," and drove off.

But surely Scotland was part of England ... Ag, she couldn't understand these people; she would have to speak to the official man in the kilt and if there were any problem with the money perhaps he would sort it out.

The Kibble Palace was a fairy-tale house of glass and wrought iron painted silver. In the first, smaller dome, the distant crown of a palm tree brushed against the glass top. There at the top each row of panes grew narrower, tapering until the tiny rectangles of glass turned into sharp triangles, which would, had there been sunlight, sparkle like diamonds. Fat, orange fish floated in the pond at the base of the tree. It was warm. She sat on a wooden bench, one she was sure Arthur would have sat on. It was no doubt the heat that had brought him here so often. But she would not give in to grief, would not allow her heart to howl with pain. She would get to the bottom of this; she owed it to Arthur who never, never would have killed himself.

She took out the ten-pound note. On the front, where a picture of a man labeled David Livingstone was trapped among palm leaves, it claimed to be issued by Clydesdale Bank PLC. On the back—and she flushed with shame—a naked woman was flanked on either side by naked men, captives or slaves, squatting serenely in their leg irons under palm trees.

An overdressed Arab on a camel occupied the middle ground, while in the distance a sailboat drifted on the water. Across the picture and across the plain white strip at the edge marked simply with the £10 figure, someone, the taxi man perhaps, had written in blue pen: If dat bastard Geldof don't git 'ere soon I goes eat dat camel.

Dorothy smoothed the note and put it into her wallet, carefully, in order not to crease it. What was she to make of this message? And who would write such bad English on what she now had to believe was a perfectly good note? A visiting dominie had once explained about the Bible, how the stories meant something other than what the actual words said. Then the story about the leper which he explicated turned out to mean exactly what she had always thought it to mean, and she checked with Mrs. Willemse who said the same. So if one thing did stand for another she was perfectly capable of working it out. But which figure was she to attribute the words to? Livingstone, an explorer, she remembered, but could he really be showing off his slaves? And who was Geldof? Should she substitute Arthur for Geldof, which was surely a Boer name? And geld meaning money? She flushed with shame, or was it rage, at the "bastard," which suggested that someone knew all about Arthur. But if Arthur were the victim, to be . . . oh, she would not think the monstrous thing through. The British Council man was right. She had to keep going, keep moving. The horror thickened in the heat, but she steadied herself and carried on.

In the approach to the main dome, on either side of the glass corridor, a discreet notice announced that this was South Africa. Not that she recognized many of the plants. A raggedy tree labeled Greyia seemed familiar but the Erica tree, sprinkled with icing-sugar, she had certainly never seen before. It was in blossom: a million miniature white chalices with the slenderest of brown stamens. *Camellia japonica* flowered a deep pink that Arthur loved. He would have come in from the biting cold into this brilliance of heat and pink. And recognized, perhaps from his books, the lilies, nerine, strelitzia, agapanthus, and of course hen and chickens posing under a posh name. She said the names of the flowers aloud in Arthur's measured tone. And she heard his new black shoes on the floor of bricks packed into neat chevrons as he followed the lure of the heat into the dome.

Palm trees squashed together in the inner circle, and from the wrought iron beams drops of condensation plopped into the dome of silence. Dorothy unbuttoned her coat. She turned right into the outer circle through Australia, New Zealand, a South American jungle, the undergrowth of temperate Asia, the Canaries, and the Mediterranean. How quickly she tread the entire world, for in no time she was back at the icing-sugared Erica, entering South Africa again.

It was in his fourth letter that Arthur spoke of lithops, of the hot stony beds where they kept prickly pears and other succulents. She found the room and smiled at the Namaqua vygies, made up, like platteland girls in Town, sitting pertly behind glass if you please.

But she knew nothing of the reed and timber hut that beckoned from another room. Its walls were lined with boards displaying texts and photographs of the Trades House of the Glasgow Expedition to Papua New Guinea. There were pictures of bearded White men with rucksacks walking through forests or bending over indistinguishable plants. Then Dorothy gasped, for there before her very eyes was Arthur, poring over a table of uprooted plants. His spread right hand was held out as if in blessing over the collection. The caption called him the High Commissioner for Papua New Guinea. Dorothy held on to the wooden post. Oh, she could have sworn it was Arthur, her own boy, tall and slender, but she supposed the man was somewhat older. Why was this photograph of a Black man mounted here to break her heart? She would not look again at this High Commissioner, and she felt a chill creep up from her feet and spread through her entire body. But she carried on, now stiff with cold. As the man from the British Council said, there was nothing to do but to carry on. She read out the text on the next board, loudly, like a child learning to read:

"... to seek out orchids, begonias and ferns for display

at the Glasgow Garden Festival and, thereafter, to become part of the permanent collection maintained at the Glasgow Botanic Gardens, part of the cultural heritage of the City."

Dorothy sank to the earth floor of the Papua New Guinea hut, leaned her head against a wooden post and spread out her legs comfortably. A young child came upon her and skipped to and fro between those legs and shouted, "Mum, look a Papoo person," but his mother whispered "Shush" and dragged him away. It was ten minutes later that a guard took her by the arm and lifted her to her feet. She did not brush the dust from her navy blue coat. What did it matter? She knew that Arthur had been swallowed by this city, that he would never again pick a thread from her lapel—Always look your best Mamma. Always look your best. Still she held her head high. But she could not answer the uniformed man's questions. He spoke softly, kindly, and she handed over her handbag to him. So he called a taxi, which took her back to the hotel.

Months later, leaning over the shop counter and peering into the heart of a cloud shaped like a camel, Dorothy could have sworn that the man had spoken to her in Afrikaans. Why did she remember the words, "Alles sal regkom Mevrou,"* but she could of course not be sure.

---

* "It will all work out in the end" in Afrikaans.

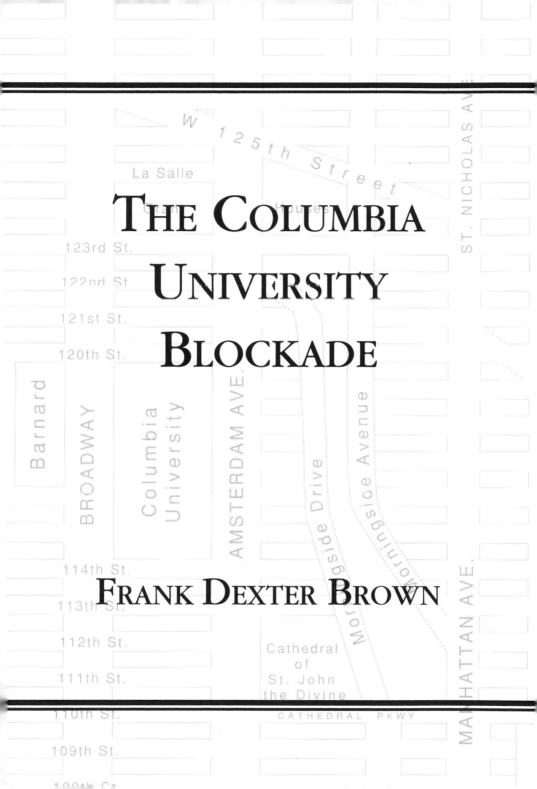

THE COLUMBIA

UNIVERSITY

BLOCKADE

FRANK DEXTER BROWN

F rank Dexter Brown has covered the South African liberation struggle extensively. As project director and cofounder of the Frontline States Media Project, an independent news agency funded by the United Nations, Brown traveled to southern Africa in 1985 and reported on the African National Congress of South Africa and the South West Africa People's Organization of Namibia. He also has written extensively on the U.S. anti-apartheid movement, in which he has been an organizer and a lobbyist.

In addition, Brown has taught at both the high school and college level over the past ten years. His articles have been published in the *Amsterdam News*, *Black Enterprise*, *Essence*, *Emerge*, and *Village Voice*, among others.

Mr. Brown is the editor of a new monthly magazine, *YSB*, directed to African American youth. He lives in Washington, D.C.

*I*f there is no struggle, there is no progress....Power concedes nothing without a demand. It never did and it never will.
—Frederick Douglass

In November 1984, South Africa was in a state of siege. The country had been brought almost to a standstill by demonstrations. Over 250,000 Black students refused to attend classes. Workers in most of the major industries followed the students' lead and participated in a workforce "stayaway." Several Black townships erupted over government-imposed rent increases. Throughout the country, *Amandla* and *Ngawethu*—the Zulu words for "power" and "to the people"—could be heard as the green, black, and gold flag of the then-banned African National Congress (ANC) was unfurled in direct defiance of apartheid laws.

The South African regime responded with a harsh reprisal code named "Operation Bullrush." The South African Defense Force* entered the townships, with devastating results: more than 200,000 homes were searched and ransacked; 4,000 people were detained without charge; 200 killed; and more than 1,000 injured. Expressions of horror came from around the world as the number of casualties grew daily. At an emergency meeting of the United Nations Security Council, only one country did not condemn the regime's actions: The United States stood alone.

American anti-apartheid groups had been attempting for some time to influence changes in United States policy

---

* South African Defense Force—the South African army.

toward South Africa. In the wake of the increased repression in South Africa, they expanded their protest actions. Anti-apartheid sentiment was spreading in the U.S.

At that time, few Americans were aware of the extent of U.S. investments in South Africa. Few knew, for instance, that one of President Ronald Reagan's first foreign policy decisions was to establish close links with South Africa. In his first public statement on apartheid, in March 1981, Reagan announced the formation of a strategic alliance with South Africa as part of his policy of "constructive engagement." These ties troubled anti-apartheid activists, who argued that without support from the U.S. government and corporations the South African regime would have found it difficult to maintain its repressive policies. In the fall of 1984, Columbia University had over $35 million worth of investments in South Africa-related holdings.

That fall, Rob Jones was a student at Columbia University. He was a member of the Black Students Organization (BSO) and was also on the steering committee of the Coalition for a Free South Africa, a vocal anti-apartheid campus group founded by the BSO in 1982. Jones had gained his political experience while in high school as a draft counselor and in college as a member of Students Against Militarism, which questioned the portion of the U.S. budget allocated to military as against domestic spending priorities. He recalls the Coalition's earliest anti-apartheid activities : "It was a step-by-step process that began with a small group of Black students. At the early stage they were involved in trying to force Columbia to divest itself of its South African holdings."

From 1982 to 1984, the Coalition for a Free South Africa undertook educational efforts on campus, showing anti-apartheid films, inviting visiting representatives from the

President Reagan's announcement of establishing closer ties with South Africa was followed by an expansion of both public and private economic, diplomatic, and military relations. From 1981 to 1985, U.S. investments grew from an aggregate $2.3 billion to $15 billion. U.S. bank loans increased by more than 167%. U.S. export of munitions also leaped, from $25,000 in 1981 to $28.3 million in 1983. In 1981-1982, U.S. corporations shipped to South Africa approximately $1.7 million of "nonmilitary" arms and ammunition, including 2,500 "shock batons" (used in the U.S. to herd cattle), whips, and electronic sensors, all of which were used by the South African police to attack Blacks. By 1985, U.S. corporations had significant influence on the most vital sectors of the South African economy, controlling 40% of its automobile industry, 48% of its oil industry, and 70% of its computer industry.

African National Congress (ANC) to speak, leafleting on campus, and initiating petition drives. They also drafted and lobbied for two consecutive resolutions requiring the university to divest itself of holdings in South African companies. Both were passed in the University Senate, one of Columbia's highest policy-making bodies, composed of administrators, faculty, and elected student representatives. Despite this evidence of increasing anti-apartheid sentiment on campus, however, university President Michael Sovern vetoed both divestment resolutions and the board of trustees refused to implement them.

The Coalition thereby explored and exhausted all the avenues for change that the university structure provided. They realized that to be successful they would need greater backing.

"South Africa was a new issue for many of the students," says Jones. "Organizing was like trying to build a house. You can't put the roof up until you have laid a foundation, put up the walls, and have the beams running. You can't have a blockade, take over a building, and engage in mass action that calls for sacrifice until you have built an organization and a following. We tried to make sure in our meetings that the students got an adequate grounding in what was taking place in South Africa and then connected it to what was happening in the U.S. We made sure that they knew the basics: where South Africa is, what apartheid is, what happens to Blacks under apartheid, and what the racist minority regime is. Then we would add, 'Do you know that Columbia is involved in supporting this system?' Students would get riled up and want to do something."

As student support increased, Jones notes, "it also became clear that the Coalition needed to be a multiracial organization. We had a majority African American leadership, with a mix of Whites and Asians."

For the members of the Coalition in 1984, a primary question was who should control the university? Wasn't it students' money, in part, that paid for the academic programs and for the salaries of faculty and administrators? And wasn't it wrong that their money was invested in corporations that supported apartheid? Shouldn't the university invest with a conscience? Thus, the struggle they fought was one of principle. Says Jones, "A question developed: How does one who is dis-empowered impact on a large and powerful institution? In this connection, questions of democracy and freedom of speech were vital. That was one reason that it was important for us to exhaust all our options through the university's processes. We could then say: 'What's the message we're supposed to get? How are we supposed to react when your response is always to say, "We'll set up a committee and talk about it"?'" By December 1984, despite two and a half years of dedicated effort, the Coalition saw that their efforts urging Columbia to divest its holdings in

South African corporations had had little impact on university policy.

In January 1985, the repression continued in South Africa. The members of the Coalition returned from the winter break with a renewed sense of urgency. Jones explains, "We'd been through all the processes. The university had just set up another committee for us to sit on. We began to feel that the vibrancy and strength the movement had had was missing. If you don't have something to show to the people you're appealing to other than sitting on a committee, people are going to lose interest. How do you keep something going without visible signs of success?"

The Coalition steering committee met several times in February to decide on a fresh, more militant approach. Jones describes the sessions: "We discussed what needed to be done. Someone said, 'We'll picket President Sovern's house,' but that had been done before. 'We'll break windows,' someone else suggested, but it was agreed that no, that didn't make sense, people wouldn't take us seriously. 'Well, we'll just have to take over a building,' someone else said."

Finally, they had it, an action that fit with Columbia's progressive student activist tradition. For in 1968 Columbia students had made national headlines when they seized and occupied Hamilton Hall, site of both classrooms and the college deans' offices. They had demanded and secured changes in university policy, including improved treatment of Black students, increased recruitment of Black students and faculty, and development of courses on Black history and culture.

The steering committee members agreed to the idea of taking over Hamilton Hall. However, they could not assume that student support would be sufficient to occupy the building as in 1968. Instead, they agreed, they would blockade the building. Further, the steering committee realized that for the blockade to be successful the plans needed to be kept confidential. It was decided that only members of the committee would know about the blockade.

The steering committee scheduled the blockade for April 4, the anniversary of the assassination of Dr. Martin Luther King, Jr. They decided to tie their action to a mass demonstration that was already planned that would feature speakers from the ANC, the South West Africa People's Organization (SWAPO), other anti-apartheid groups, and faculty and student speakers.

With little over a month to prepare, the steering committee mapped out the logistics required to take over the building. "It was like something out of 'I Spy'," says Jones, recalling the 1960s television show. "Reconnaissance teams went into Hamilton Hall, noticing very carefully how the doors opened, where the hinges were, whether or not the handles were close enough to be chained closed, and how long the chains needed to be . . . I remember people going to the roof to see how we could deal with a SWAT team if they brought one in."

Since the blockade of Hamilton Hall was to occur while classes were in session, they also had to ensure that exits were available for students, faculty, and administrators to leave Hamilton Hall after the blockade began. A series of underground tunnels connect many of the buildings on campus. The steering committee decided to post signs and have monitors ready to guide people out of Hamilton Hall through the tunnels so that they would not be accused of creating a fire hazard or jeopardizing the safety of those in the building.

When the day arrived, they were ready.

"We divided into groups—two or three people were responsible for organizing and carrying out the demonstration, others for being in the building, in the tunnels, and elsewhere, and some for relaying signals between the demonstrators and the people at Hamilton Hall. I was one of the people waiting inside the building. The blockade was to begin on a specific chant by the demonstrators.

"After the rally the demonstrators marched around campus and then on to Hamilton Hall. At the signal, we went about securing the building. The doors were chained. The steering committee members took up positions in front of the building. Other demonstrators quickly realized what was happening and joined in."

Demonstrators swarmed on the steps of Hamilton Hall. Inside, as classes let out, monitors directed people out of the building. Just like that, the building was theirs.

"After the university had spent years ignoring the students, we were in control," Jones recalls. "The university did nothing. They were extraordinarily afraid of bad publicity. So they let us stay. If they had taken a different tack and called security immediately, they could have shut it down very quickly, very easily, without the kind of publicity they got in '68 when police beat students' heads and there was blood. After a couple of hours Dean Pollack of the College came out and said: 'Listen, this is not a good thing. You shouldn't do this. You're breaking the rules.' And then he sent campus security to tell us the same thing."

"Our response was, 'We've done it now. You'd better tell us something besides what we can or cannot do.' Now we had their building. Now we owned that place."

The steering committee was ebullient. Not only had they planned something that was successful, but there had been no leaks.

"We had done a lot of thinking and planning beforehand," says Jones. "However, our plans stopped at the point when the building was chained and all the people sat down. Yes, there had been debates about how long the action would last: Some believed three hours, others—a very small faction—said three days. Once the blockaders were actually in place and the demonstrators decided to cast their lot with us, we were completely unprepared for what was to happen next. That was the end of our plan. We had thought that something would go wrong with the plan, that security and the administration would break it up. Or that the demonstrators would say, 'This is crazy. We're not going to sit with them.' That wasn't the case, of course. So there we were, 14 or so planners on the Coalition steering committee (most of whom were Black), immediately supported by 75 to 100 people (most of whom were White). That's when things began to get interesting."

Immediately, the steering committee met to decide how to proceed. They gathered in the Malcolm X Lounge. Throughout the next few weeks the lounge served as the command center of the blockade.

"The first thing that had to happen," Jones explains, "was organizing food for people, as well as blankets for the people who were planning to spend the night at the blockade site—one of the most memorable things about the first few days is how cold it was. We also had to organize security; we had the perimeter of the place staked out each way for about 100 yards. We also had to tell people what the implications were, that real risks were involved. For those of us on the steering committee, the level of our responsibility started coming through."

Up to that moment the Coalition steering committee had made all decisions, but with the building secured, Jones says, ". . . spontaneous, spur of the moment, brilliant, see-a-need-and-fulfill-it kinds of things took place. Out of nowhere people came with coats and blankets. Students living in the Hartley Hall dormitory, adjacent to Hamilton Hall, made their suite available to us, and it became both our kitchen and our press office. Student writers became part of a press crew, preparing news releases. Computer-oriented people set up networks and billboards through which they communicated with other colleges. It was amazing. It seemed as if people were just waiting for something like this to tap into."

As students dispatched news releases and the word got out, press organizations began to flood the protest site.

Additionally, residents from the Harlem community offered their support. Historically, there had been few ties between Harlemites and Columbia students, despite their geographic proximity. Some students, many of them members of the BSO, had been involved in neighborhood campaigns for tenants fighting Columbia the landlord. (Columbia is one of the largest landlords in Harlem and has extensive real estate holdings throughout New York.) As in 1968, Harlem residents found the blockade of the "students on the hill" a positive and courageous act. Sylvia Woods, owner of the internationally famous Sylvia's Restaurant on Lenox Avenue, sent a truckload of chicken and other food to students on the second day of the protest. Sylvia was in the hospital when she heard a news report on WLIB, the city's Black news and talk radio station, which was first to cover the protest. Says Jones of Sylvia's efforts and those of other community supporters: "People in the Harlem community view Columbia as an outside presence. But when they saw us protest in support of Black South Africans and against the university, they were supportive. We were told by some residents that through our protests they also voiced their objections to the university for imposing itself on the Harlem community and not reinvesting in the community."

Other organizations were equally supportive. "While we didn't have a lot of experience with the trade unions, a representative from District Council 37 of AFSCME told us that they were behind us 100% and whatever we needed they would try to get. We told them tarps, blankets, and money. The next day a flatbed truck pulled up on College

Walk [the main roadway that cuts through the middle of campus] with tarps, blankets, and a check for $500."

The sight of the goods being unloaded aroused the interest of other students. "We didn't know anything about setting up tarps," says Jones, "but up came some students who were engineers and others who were architects who offered to put them up. Other students saw how plain the tarps looked and said, 'We can't put them up like that,' and they started making protest signs and placards. They painted the tarps in the black, green, and gold of the ANC and printed *Amandla* and *Ngawethu* across them. Within three days there was a heavy rain. There were a few leaks, but everyone was dry."

The demonstrators encamped around the steps of Hamilton Hall were highly visible as well as audible. In addition, a number of classes usually held in the building were unofficially relocated. Despite that, the university administration acted as if nothing were happening. Says Jones: "It was a bizarre dynamic. The administration's attitude was 'The children are misbehaving.' They still hadn't figured out the power of the blockade. By the time they did, it was much too late. By the end of the first week we were so entrenched that folks were ready to have their heads beaten, get arrested, or be thrown out of school." Many students slept and ate at the blockade site. Students also took turns attending classes, to ensure that a minimum of twenty to thirty people was always present at the site.

The quadrangle in which Hamilton Hall is located became an active university within a university, as steering committee members and local activists held "classes" every evening on the evils of apartheid and racism in society in general. Jesse Jackson and other national and local political leaders came to speak. Performers such as Don Cherry and Pete Seeger taught through "political art," entertaining with their music, discussing the blockade and its place in the greater history of the progressive movement, and encouraging the demonstrators. Telegrams of support were received from student groups and individuals in Germany, Italy, and Japan, among others.

Says Jones: "Political education was important and served to keep us going over the days and weeks. A key reason we continued these sessions was that the blockade reflected the student population at Columbia—the majority of participants were White. As time went on, we were drawing more and more parallels between racism in South Africa and in the United States, between those who live in South African 'townships' and those who live in their U.S. equivalents, such as Harlem in New York City and Watts in Los Angeles. Many students were hearing such things for the first time and broke down in tears. For them, the blockade served as an awakening. To a degree, we were involved in the untraining of racist behavior."

It was now late April, and the blockade was in its third week. Within two weeks it would be final exam time, and shortly thereafter, graduation. The mood at the blockade began to change. Jones explains, "People started getting frightened about being thrown out of school, what they were going to do, and how they were going to respond if the police came."

Sensing the change in attitudes, the steering committee began to discuss whether to end the blockade. Although the university administration had not agreed to divest itself of its holdings, there had been some breakthroughs. For the first time university officials had been forced to take the Coalition seriously: By the second week, President Sovern had held his first meeting ever with the group, and students had also met with President Ellen Futter of Barnard College, Columbia's private and independent sister institution. Moreover, bonds had been established with the Harlem community, the trade unions, the city's anti-apartheid community and other colleges nationally. Most important, the Columbia action had sparked anti-apartheid activism throughout the country.

The steering committee was divided on whether the blockade should end. "One bloc said we should go on," says Jones. "Through exams, through graduation, through the summer, through to the fall and the next semester. 'We'll just go,' they said. They believed people would continue to support us because they had supported us this long.

"The other group argued that there was no way the support would continue indefinitely, that we had been lucky and had strained our resources to the breaking point. Now to ask people to give up their final exams, basically to fail their exams, in addition to taking whatever discipline the university might impose, was excessive. Besides, there would be no campus support during the summer when few of the students would be in school."

As in all their deliberations, the steering committee remained democratic and respectful of all opinions. Says Jones: "We viewed ourselves as a unit, even if there were disagreements. This camaraderie and respect allowed us to work through our political differences."

They agreed to declare a tactical victory and to put the university on notice that if it did not divest they would be back. The steering committee decided to close the protest by holding a march and rally, and to do so in Harlem, because of the message it would send to their Harlem friends and the university in general. "We understood that we couldn't have done this without the support of the Harlem community," Jones explains. "Their energy, their time, their food, their money, their solidarity was constant."

By this time, however, the steering committee was fighting to maintain control. "For some time, low-level tension had existed between the committee and some students over the issue of Black leadership of the blockade, which was composed predominantly of Whites," Jones explains. When the steering committee announced the march and rally in Harlem and asked the demonstrators to vote on it, that tension surfaced.

Some students argued, and some others agreed, that the protest should end with a rally at Columbia, saying that those from the Harlem community could attend if they wished, but that their participation during the blockade had not been vital. "It is our event. They should come to us," was the sentiment expressed.

"The impact of this on individual members of the steering committee was extraordinary," says Jones. "A number of us were ready to just walk away. Our response was, damn it, after all we'd gone through, the way we had struggled over issues. We felt we had wasted our time and that all the political education—particularly education on the parallels between racism in the U.S. and South Africa— had been thrown to the dogs."

Still, they couldn't give up. Instead, they appealed to the assembled demonstrators one last time. Each member of the steering committee made a statement. "We spoke as a united front and addressed the issue of racism and the principles of the Coalition. We spoke about the group's founding and our work over the years. We reminded the demonstrators that Harlemites *had* come to us: It was because of their support that the blockade was able to last as long as it did. Now, we said, it was our turn to go to them. We were very firm. People were devastated. And then the floodgates opened as people began to cry. It was agreed that we would march and rally in Harlem."

Twenty-six days after the protest had begun, over 1,000 protesters—students, faculty, community activists—made their way from the campus down through Morningside Park to 125th Street and to New Canaan Baptist Church, long a haven for the city's progressive activists and for the

ANC and SWAPO. Jones tells of the jubilance of the day: "We marched holding high the chains that had been used to lock the doors. There were placards and banners and the flags of the ANC and SWAPO, and along the streets people called to us in support. Some joined us. On we went. Finally, at New Canaan we held a rally. Then we marched again to Columbia and had another rally and a party."

Their protest did, in fact, continue through to the graduation ceremony. At an agreed upon moment 200 graduates flashed signs on their graduation caps that read "Divest Now" and walked out on the ceremony. At the same time, although totally independently, other students made their way to the top of Butler Library and unfurled banners that also demanded divestiture.

After all the work, the message had indeed been heard. Within a few months, Columbia announced its decision to divest itself of holdings in companies that did business in South Africa.

Today, some six years later, Rob Jones still describes the experience as one of the most important of his life. He says that the members of the steering committee remain close and that they and other blockade participants continue to be involved in movement work. "I keep running into people who were involved in the blockade who are working with alternative newspapers and radio stations, with tenant organizations, soup kitchens, or the homeless. People really did get the message. A lot of people gained an understanding that there is an alternative to the status quo, that there is an alternative to buying into the system."

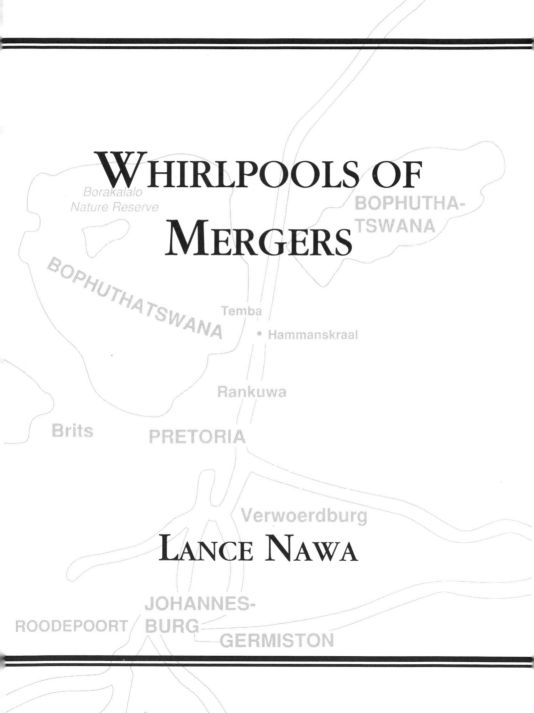

WHIRLPOOLS OF MERGERS

LANCE NAWA

Photo by Themba Nkosi

Lance Nawa was born in Lady Selbourne, a racially integrated neighborhood of Pretoria. When Lady Selbourne was razed because it violated apartheid laws, Mr. Nawa's family moved to Hammanskraal. After high school, he received a bachelor's degree with honors in sociology from the University of Cape Town.

Mr. Nawa is the author of *Muso—Poetry Perched on Live Wires*. His articles have been featured in several publications, including *Ingolovane, New Nation, Staffrider, Upbeat,* and the *Weekly Mail*. He is currently a writer at *Bona* magazine and chairperson of the Transvaal Regional Office of the Congress of South African Writers.

Mr. Nawa lives in Pretoria.

*T*he following story is a parable about apartheid. The setting, a
small village, exhibits apartheid's trademark, the centrifugal
separation and scattering of people along racial and ethnic lines.
Simultaneously, it bespeaks the drawing together of South
Africans of all races—despite the barriers between them—by the
centripetal force of their shared humanity. The story points to
the ethnic and jurisdictional antipathies at play in a village on the
border between South Africa and the "independent homeland" of
Bophuthatswana, which has its own government, police force,
army and flag. The picture Nawa presents is a microcosm of the
South African struggle for a nonracial unitary state, one that no
longer features a system of separate "homelands."

It was in the afternoon, a few hours before sunset, and
the atmosphere was humid. The sun stood so still I could
actually feel individual rays stabbing at my back as I
made my way from the dam where I had been sitting—I
don't care to remember for what reason. Trees also stood
motionless, in rows, like soldiers called to attention by a
fiery superior.

This stillness belied the dazzling world I had just experienced at the dam: the jumping, racing, circling, waving,
chirping, and gulling of lives around the riverside. I was
frantically trying to conduct the unruly orchestra of sounds
into a single refreshing melody when shouts jabbed me
into reality. "Look out! Look out!" I felt as if I were waking
up to a vigorous slapping by an evangelical fanatic or a
bearded imam trying to drive demons out of my system.
But it did not take a holy spirit to know that the warning
was not for me. Or perhaps it was . . .

Not far from where I stood, a commotion of people was
parading under tall bluegum trees, like chickens that had
just had their eggs stolen or snatched by a vulture. They
were hurling stones into one of the trees queued into a

147

single straight line on the left side of the road running through Hammanskraal.

This road, coming from Pretoria and stretching to the north, bisected Hammanskraal at this point like the hand of an erratic surgeon. To the left, beyond the trees, were a few small houses; a set of railroad tracks; the dam I had just come from; and beyond that the Temba township, all laid out proportionately. On the right, smoldering like a huge snuffed candle, was the village of Marokolong. The whole hung like a painting by a schizophrenic artist. The different brush strokes appeared to resist a merger of any sort.

When I was a boy, Temba township harbored the Mathulatshipis and the Mazakhelas, two groups of boys who derived sensuous pleasure and power-affirmation from clubbing each other with an assortment of sticks. Whether the bone of contention was merely a territorial matter over zones within the township, or something deeply rooted in the politics of the country, I never lived there long enough to find out. (Any knowledge of the place I may now hold I owe to history books and my personal analysis.)

Marokolong, across the river, was also a unique puzzle. My then small mind could not come to grips with its ethnically charged territorial references like "Shangaan Street" and "Matabeleng." Nor with the fact that some of the people of Marokolong, for purposes of greeting, used to extend their walking sticks for the Tsonga-speaking people to grasp, when handshakes were by far the most warm, friendly, and immediate recognition of existence.

The river had passed between these two antagonistic areas for generations, a buffer zone and the arena for my childhood adventures and duels. I and other boys from the two opposing villages used to deploy ourselves on both banks and engage in mud-slinging and stone-throwing. The victors would get the honor of swimming in the water to the envy of the losers, until the next showdown. Fishing lines were cast from either side of the river, only to hook and weave themselves into knots in the middle of whirlpools.

That was before one part of the river was converted into a huge dam (now called Temba beach) supplying Temba with sanitary water and electricity. Marokolong remained a dry pit.

On innumerable occasions the boys of my village made me account for my family's funny accent, our odd *boesman** features and curly hair (which was carefully concealed under a *doekie* or sometimes adorned with colorful ribbons or rollers by female members of the family). And every time I tried to unravel this mystery, it deepened instead. My mother's dismissive attitude toward my questioning did not help the situation.

For all my inquisitiveness, the only answer I could get from my lovely mother about matters of ethnicity was that any discussion of my parched fair-skinned ancestry— already mummified into very pale images in the family portraits I found one day hidden in a box—was impotent and could only be redeemed by my aspirations for a non-racial society. My grandmother's famous and petite "Queen Elizabeth's nose" was to be forgotten, and the legend of Queen Madjodji** remembered. All I needed to survive, my mother said, was for my tongue to speak not Afrikaans but Sepedi; my heart to pound like a drum from the River Nile; and my veins to course with the blood of Sekhukhure, Shaka, Steve Biko, and even Marcus Garvey.

In fact, she made things worse, for many times I sneaked in on her and caught her listening to the Afrikaans "Springbok Radio" or reading Afrikaans literature, in-

---

* boesman—Afrikaans word for "Colored."
** Queen Madjodji—The ruling monarch of a region in northern Transvaal known for her rainmaking powers.

cluding sleazy and propaganda-packed comics like *Kyk*, *Die Wit Tier*, and *Die Grens Vegter*. The latter two were the most amazing (when I could lay my hands on them undetected, that is), for they portrayed successful one-man crusades against the forces of devil and darkness (communist terrorists) who were out to overthrow some democratic government in Africa. Completing these missions was every boy's dream, for the hero always ended up in the romantic company of a vivacious woman in a scanty bikini.

It was at that time that more families moved into our village, like the Moseses and Laarts, who appeared to have been baked in the same confused biographical ovens as my family—District Six, Sophiatown, Marabastad, and so forth.* They put up near our house. I deliberately shunned their attempts to befriend us. I was not at all keen on seeing myself in them. I joined the other boys of the community in their hospitable task of welcoming the strangers with stone-throwing and the subsequent demanding of "protection fees."

With time, all of these ethnic hostilities simmered down. We became birds of a feather. We hunted, fished, gathered wild fruit, and played football against teams from neighboring communities. And how could I forget the rustling sound the grass made under our weight as we nestled down with girls to enjoy the sweet innocence of youth?

These were signs of good things to come, but I came back to the place almost too late, as a visitor, to notice them happening. All the same it had been inspiring to sit at the dam and reminisce without the fear that I might have to defend myself with a *slaanver* or *kettie*. In any case,

---

*These surnames and geographical references indicate mixed racial origins.

the river had by now been caged into a dam that was far too wide for stones or mud to fly across.

I now crossed the road and settled myself on a patch of grass to watch the immediate unfolding spectacle, my back turned to Marokolong, smoldering and decaying like a wedding cake not eaten for ages. From this angle, the dam, the railroad tracks, and Temba township cast an image of obscured realities through the monstrous trees. The only living background was the sun's rays sieving through the branches.

Across the road, a volley of stones shot skyward into one of the trees, striking a branch that overhung, or rather dangled over, the middle of the road. The ground underneath had become carpeted with pieces of brown granite material. People swarmed the place. Hands went for every stone in the vicinity. Even stones that were firmly in the ground were unearthed. Projectiles kept flying into the tree, pausing only at the drone of passing cars.

A viper was engaged in a fight for life. It clung to the swaying branch, praying that this lethal target practice must fail. A few motorists stopped their vehicles alongside the road and joined in the offensive. The branch then seemed to throw in the towel. Like a stunned boxer, it sank, only to be slapped skyward by the top of each passing car. Drivers who saw the reptile at the eleventh hour ducked their heads and slammed on their brakes. The squeal of tires and the gasoline fumes made the human organism cringe.

Then the constitutional aspect of the episode emerged, though no pounding of a gavel was heard. One of the rock throwers suggested that some sort of legal counsel might be necessary to avoid complications. However, the person in question had to jump some jurisdictional hurdles before he could come to a concrete suggestion, for the territorial authority over Marokolong fell uncertainly between South Africa and Bophuthatswana.

He first considered running to the nearest police station, but could not bring himself to respond to the immediate beckoning of the South African Police flag. The only option left, of which he promptly availed himself, was a police station flying the blue and orange flag of Bophuthatswana. The flag fluttered excitedly as if to say:

> Welcome to the land of Your Excellency,
> the Honorable Doctor, Moporesidente,
> Kgosi Kgolo, Motlotlegi, Tau-tona,
> Mr. Lucas Mangope*

It was about an hour's walk to that building, symbol of a bloodless independence, and half that time for a fiery Olympic runner. Our legal hero let his heels bang the back of his head as he raced against the clock.

Indeed, developments needing legal counsel unfolded a few minutes after he took off. A White motorist who had stepped out of his car was suddenly the one being pelted with stones. The reason? He had suggested that the serpent be left alone, for he knew of some technological apparatus with which it could be captured without hassles, alive even. But he quickly learned that carnivores do not need utensils when tearing meat for lunch. Like a dog with its tail between its legs, he hurried back to his car and sped off.

Then another incident occurred that commuted the viper's death sentence a little longer.

A vehicle was running mad on the road like a wounded Spanish bull. The driver of the car had apparently collapsed onto the steering wheel at the sight of the cold-blooded animal dangling in front of the windshield as if it were going to fly right into the car's interior. The car zigzagged along the road and finally swerved into the

---

*President of Bophuthatswana.

opposite lane, promising a head-on collision with an on-coming one. At that juncture all that could be heard was the screeching, bursting, splintering, and clapping of glass, rubber, and metal as the cars slammed into each other.

The atmosphere was eerie. Hands froze around stones. Faces masked a ghost town. But like actors under the spell of a famous movie director, the people united in simultaneous action and hurried to the wreckage. It could clearly be seen, amid the blood-stained bodies and clothes, that the occupants of the two cars were Black and White, respectively. All the same, victims were victims; they were to be treated accordingly.

The sun was still bidding the "extras" a farewell when sirens pierced the air like a hot knife through butter. The noise grew so loud that it did not take a hearing specialist to notice that a convoy of ambulances, fire extinguishers, and police vans was announcing its arrival.

The crowd promptly went into action like medics at the scene of war casualties. They put one of the injured Black women onto a stretcher and lifted her into an ambulance. They were about to make a second delivery of a White victim when they were stopped and sternly warned about "his own ambulance." Many naive observers envied the crash victim for his apparent wealth, for owning even an ambulance. The Black police of Bophuthatswana and the White police of South Africa tried to untangle this jurisdictional knot with a touch of professionalism. Every-thing was done so amicably that if there were psychologi-cal strains between them they were not noticed. (Until later that night, that is, when like owls these two strange bedfellows went around, separately, to interrogate anyone involved with any part of the rock-throwing incident.)

Exit the supporting action. The viper seemed to have gained courage, energy, and momentum. People followed its movements as if watching a trapeze artist in action or a live tennis match. It became defiant. It raised its head as if to strike and shook it menacingly. It was furious, hissing survival tactics at the spectators. Boys were separated from men, girls from women, the coward from the brave. Many scurried off. Safety meant fleeing in a stampede. The spectacle was like a film about payday in South Africa.

People's ears danced staccato to the stuttering of guns. Cr-a-aaack! The branch around which the viper had roped itself fell to the ground with a deafening thud like the collapsing castles of absolute rulers. Blood from its head wound squirted like the river of early battles that flows across the pages of South African history books.

The precise origin of the accurate bullet was never known. Only a legacy of competing claims remained over who had fired the successful shot, but it would become clear that the ammunition was fired from a single, or rather common, barrel.

The mournful sun lolled its head, sinking into its orange blanket, and disappeared . . .

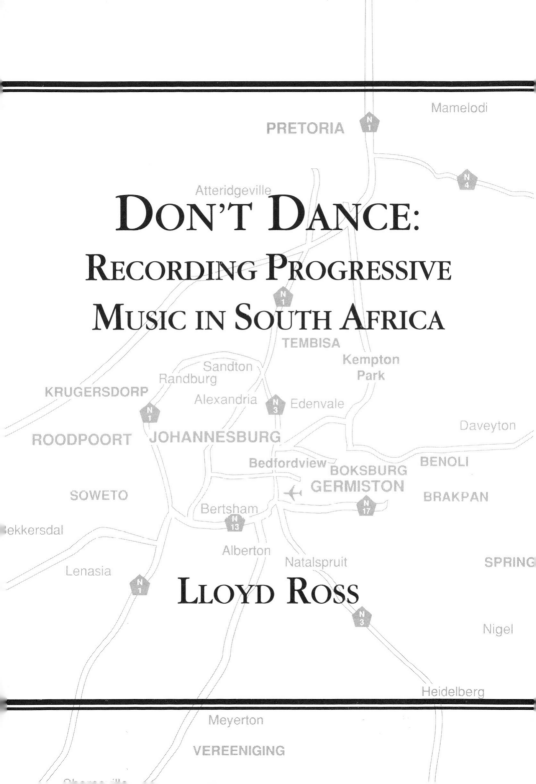

DON'T DANCE:
RECORDING PROGRESSIVE
MUSIC IN SOUTH AFRICA

LLOYD ROSS

Lloyd Ross was born in Cape Town. After high school he fulfilled his military requirement by serving in the South African Navy for two years.

Mr. Ross briefly worked at the South African Broadcasting Corporation in Johannesburg and later became a member of the band Radio Rats. Working as a sound engineer in the film industry, he saved enough money to buy music equipment. In 1980, he and Ivan Kadey founded Shifty Records, the only South African production company to record alternative noncommercial music. Since that time he has been a music producer and has worked with musicians and groups such as Mzwakhe Mbuli, Sankomoto, and the Kalahari Surfers.

Mr. Ross lives in Johannesburg.

I had an upbringing not dissimilar to that of a large majority of White South Africans: White friends, White school, cultural influence mainly filtered Anglo-American. The discos and clubs I went to were segregated; theaters, cinemas, even the radio stations were to a large degree reserved for American and British music, with the occasional White local band getting airtime. If it weren't for so many Black people on the street and a sneaky air of authoritarianism, you would have sworn you were in some secure European democracy. So efficient were the propaganda organs of the state that one felt that Goebbels could have learned something from the ruling National Party (as surely as they did from him).

This was apartheid: simply that people of different color shall be kept separate in all ways possible. For more than forty years, the Government of South Africa explained to the rest of the world, this was because people of different races wanted to preserve their own culture and identity and therefore did not want to live together. So much for the marketed image, because built into the grand scheme was, of course, the fact that all privilege was reserved exclusively for Whites: best residential areas, jobs, beaches, entertainment venues, toilets, park benches, etc., etc., etc.

Growing up in a stable environment, I came to view my world as normal. It was only as I grew older and developed the propensity for questioning the major issues of life that I was actually able to begin changing my prejudices. The impressions of injustice did filter through the distractions of youth, however. I remember, for instance, often wondering why a Black man the same age as my father was never accorded the same sort of respect.

That was the world I emerged from when I got out of

compulsory institutions (schooling, military service) in
1976–77. It was a time of great turmoil in the country, with
the Soweto riots and a prevalent feeling of instability and
paranoia. It was also a time of musical upheaval in the
world as the punk/new wave phenomenon made its
presence felt. Punk was by definition a music of protest
against the established order, a sentiment not lost on a few
disillusioned local kids.

It was about then, returning home after spending some
time in Europe, that I walked into a club in Johannesburg
and sat down to watch a group called the Radio Rats.
Their energy and original approach to music impressed
me so much that I knew I had to play with this band. After
pestering them for half a year I finally got my way. I
then discovered a vibrant new wave scene that blossomed
through 1978 and 1979 with quality, original, honest-to-
goodness South African bands like the Asylum Kids,
Corporal Punishment, and National Wake. Over the
driving rhythms of high-energy rock music they sang
about the world around them, their country, their peers,
in a way unknown in South Africa before. The compositions and delivery were very honest, very direct:

He's got a Cortina and a Granada
He built them himself with the help of his father
Company house, company wine
He's so secure, he thinks he's divine

He's a supervisor, it takes a lot of skill
To be in charge of forty kaffirs—that's responsible
He doesn't mind when he gets all the pay
Mr. Arrie Paulus says, "They're just baboons anyway"

Brain damage

He loves to prick and to poke them
His fun is to push and provoke them

It's always such a thrill and delight
When they're too shit scared to stand up and fight

Brain damage

He looks at Arrie's car
He scrapes his feet on the tar
He marvels at his lot
Remember Egypt and the Israelites
Remember Hitler and human rights

—"Brain Damage" by Corporal Punishment

Corporal Punishment was a band from Springs, a sprawling industrial mining town near Johannesburg. In this song they characterize a White mine supervisor: where he lives, what he owns, what he thinks. The White mine union boss, Arrie Paulus, is quoted verbatim from a statement he made about his views on Black mine laborers.

It was through involvement with these people as a fellow musician that I came to learn of the frustrations of being outside the accepted norm in an abnormal society. More than you would find in, say, the United States or Europe, the establishment had a rigid and conservative way of judging people who chose to be different. That attitude was much in place in the music industry, which to all intents and purposes was blinkered when it came to making creative or aesthetic decisions about anything musical. The fate of musicians was decided exclusively on whether their songs were commercial, and that in South Africa meant whether they were played on radio.

To understand the implications of that, one must realize that the airwaves were and still are monopolized by the South African Broadcasting Corporation (SABC), which in turn is controlled by the Government. That is its chief propaganda tool. Anything that comments on the social or political status quo is immediately barred from the air. More than that, music (even instrumental) that is even slightly different from the norm does "not fit into the format" of local radio and is not playlisted. The power of this medium in any society cannot be overestimated. In music, it can make or break an artist.

The record-company type of attitude spilled over into the live music sphere. Managers, promoters, and club owners in the city venues wanted to employ only bands that played "commercial" music (music one would hear on the radio)—all the better if they covered the hit parade and played no original compositions whatever.

That is the background against which the South African new wave/alternative music scene must be visualized— not as in Europe or America, where sectors of the music industry reacted positively and creatively to the new challenge and formed a viable system of promotion and distribution, where clubs were opened up to the music and radio stations gave it cognizance and airtime.

By the end of 1980 I had had enough of seeing exciting bands come and go with the ebb and flow of their own energy, with no industry support whatever. That was the real motivation behind starting Shifty Studio. Ivan Kadey, a friend who played for National Wake, and I pooled resources and established a very basic 8-track recording studio. The facility was housed in a caravan (hence the name Shifty). The reason for the caravan was partly the free and untethered spirit that informed the project, and partly and more practically the fact that we could record anywhere in the subcontinent that we pleased. To illustrate: One of our first recordings was of the group Sankomoto in the Kingdom of Lesotho.* They were in a particularly desperate situation, having been deported

---

*Lesotho is completely surrounded by South Africa. It also has too small a population to support a professional music scene.

from South Africa while touring in 1979 and unable to return. The authorities did not take kindly to their lyric content.

The only way for members of the band to make recordings and so further their musical careers was for them to fly to another country; surface travel was out of the question because they were denied entry into South Africa. Flying would have cost the kind of money that no one had access to. Enter the studio on wheels to record Shift 001. We pulled the caravan up next to the disused Radio Lesotho studios in Maseru, the capital. A week later we had recorded our first album.

It was while trying to market those recordings that we really discovered the nature of the adversary that we had chosen to take on. The biggest discovery was that the radio stations refused to play them because the band mixes their languages. They sing in Sotho, Zulu, and English, all languages commonly heard in South Africa and languages frequently mixed, especially in the cities. Apartheid dictates, however, that different cultures shall remain "pure." Hence there is a radio station for each language, allowed to broadcast in that language only. We also could not find anyone to distribute Sankomoto's album. So what we had essentially was an album that we couldn't promote because we couldn't get it played on the radio and because the band was not allowed into South Africa to play before an audience, and an album that we couldn't get into the stores effectively because of a disinterested industry.

You can't keep good music down, however; through word of mouth the album started to sell slowly, as it is still selling almost a decade later. It was released in Europe, where the group has since toured twice. They were recently allowed into South Africa once again and have taken their deserved place as one of the most popular festival bands on the circuit.

Working with Sankomoto and encountering the problems associated with the marketing of their album, I began to realize that people outside the new wave movement were also producing alternative music. We began talking to various progressive organizations about the music produced by people with whom they came in contact. The result of this communication was two completely different compilation albums.

The first album brought together twelve separate cultural groups, mostly choirs. Each choir represented a union of the trade union giant FOSATU (Federation of South African Trade Unions). Having mobile equipment came in very useful once again, as the album was recorded at various locations around the country. We recorded in church and community halls in a number of townships, at rallies, and even in factories. The last cut on the album features a medley of popular freedom songs sung by textile workers, recorded in a storeroom during a lunch break.

That was my introduction to music with strictly political content; it was also my entry into cultural politics in a more general sense. The unions were operating under very difficult circumstances. First, they had been legalized very recently, so organizationally they were a bit unstable. Second, because of the law permitting detention without trial and later the Emergency Laws (in force from 1984 until mid-1990), many of the leaders were in prison. Those who were not were operating under the debilitating pressure of being on the run. Third, FOSATU was in the process of dissolving itself to form an even larger body, COSATU (Congress of South African Trade Unions). The launching of the album was planned for a huge rally to celebrate the birth of COSATU. At the last minute the rally was banned by the authorities; such were the times under the State of Emergency.

The second compilation album was of bands that had

played on the anticonscription platform. In South Africa only Whites are conscripted into the armed forces. The End Conscription Campaign (ECC) was formed to work against conscription, because in South Africa the army's function is primarily to defend apartheid policies. A good degree of the ECC's energies went into marketing its image and ideas through well-organized media campaigns involving posters, fetes, seminars, advertisements, demonstrations, and—of course—music gigs. Because of its high public profile, the organization attracted its fair share of more negative attention as well. Agents of the security forces undertook various dirty tricks and scare tactics. These included throwing bricks through windows in the dead of night, slashing car tires, fire-bombing houses and offices, and releasing tear gas at concerts. Other forms of harassment included smear campaigns, mostly through distribution of pamphlets. In a recent court case the South African Defense Force (SADF) was finally convicted of perpetrating such a deed.

Following are lyrics of a record from the ECC album, which was entitled *Forces Favorites*:

OK people get up off your feet
It's time to move to a different beat
We don't like the way they're running our days
And nights . . . Our lives are out of phase
We're Black/White, separated
Right from birth indoctrinated
Years and years developed apart
Brainwashed each in the name of God
Let's de-educate ourselves
Let's re-educate ourselves

Hey White boy get your feet off the floor
The Lord gave you legs to march to war
Your leaders want you in a sporting affair
So put on your boots and cut your hair

Don't talk back or stop to think
When you're in Angola you can have a drink
Obey, obey they know the way
From here you go to SWA*
Where they don't dance
When facing such hostility
They don't dance
[in a sarcastic chant:]
'Cause the SADF is there to see that we all enjoy democracy
'Cause the SAP** are there to see that we all enjoy democracy

—"Don't Dance," by the Kalahari Surfers

One day toward the end of that recording project, in late 1985, one of the ECC organizers came to the studio with a tall man from Soweto. This was Mzwakhe Mbuli, who later came to be known as "the People's Poet." I had encountered him before at a cultural evening organized by a Johannesburg progressive organization. On that occasion I was impressed with his charismatic delivery of his poetry. His words were very direct. I thought it might be interesting to get him together with some musicians. The idea was for them to provide a musical background for Mbuli's poetry, thus making it more accessible in recorded form. I discussed the idea with him, and a short time later we sat down in the studio with three musicians and workshopped some poems into songs. The experiment worked so well that these recordings were later included in an

---

*SWA—South West Africa, now independent Namibia. The United Nations ended the South African mandate over South West Africa in October 1966. The continued administration of the territory by South Africa from 1966 to 1989 was not recognized by the U.N. In 1989, after twenty-three years of war, Namibia gained its independence.
**SAP—South African Police.

album that was completed some months later. Titled *Change Is Pain*, the album was banned from distribution and possession soon after its release. When we wrote the censors asking which songs they did not like, they replied that the whole album was "inflammatory" and therefore dangerous because it could incite people to violence.

This drastic form of censorship was only too common throughout the 1980s. Anyone found in possession of banned objects faced a maximum of ten years' imprisonment, a fine up to 20,000 rand (U.S.$10,000), or both. Banned objects could include anything from literature, magazines, and records to paraphernalia emblazoned with the logo of banned organizations (of which the African National Congress was one). Great as was the demand for *Change Is Pain*, we could not afford to be seen distributing it. Blank-label copies did, however, start to appear. Also, through home taping the album made its way around the country, as was apparent at rallies where Mbuli's poems could be heard repeated word for word.

> God has given life unto man
> And man has taken life from man
> Let us say no unto slavery and mutilation
> Let us say yes unto victory and harmony
> For the spear has fallen
>
> God forgives, I don't!
> For the heart of Africa is bleeding
> Bleeding from the wounds knifed hollow
> Brutally knifed alone in the night
>
> Pick it up and forward to the battle
> Pick it up fight side by side for these freedoms
> Pick it up fight side by side for a democratic South Africa
> For the spear has fallen
> —From "The Spear Has Fallen" by Mbuli

All the people mentioned in *Change Is Pain* were political activists who had died at the hands of unknown assassins. Obviously, such assassins had an interest in maintaining the status quo. Headlined in South Africa recently was the naming of a commission of inquiry to investigate the CCB (ironically called the Civilian Cooperation Bureau), a section of the military whose activities have been proved to include death squads.

Says Mbuli about his poetry:

"Look, I don't write sonnets because I am not writing about love. I don't write odes because I'm not writing about nature. I use the language of the people, the language of the struggle, because I am writing about the people and their struggle.

"Our difference today is mobilization. . . . This is not poetry for reflection or description or comment—this is poetry for action."*

At that time Mbuli was constantly on the run from the authorities. He was detained a number of times, the longest being seven months in 1988.

After his release we decided to produce a second album, titled *Unbroken Spirit*. Most of the material in this collection was written—or rather composed and memorized, as Mbuli was not allowed pen or paper—while he was in solitary confinement. It has since achieved gold status (in South Africa that means sales of more than 25,000), even without benefit of any radio airtime.

In mid-1988 a new musical phenomenon reared its cocky head: the Afrikaans** new wave. We released a number of Afrikaans albums during that year. The most popular was by Johannes Kerkorrel en die Gereformeerde Blues Band. Literally translated, the name means Johnny

---

* "Poet of the Struggle," *Los Angeles Times*, December 1, 1987.
** Afrikaans is a Dutch-based language.

Churchorgan and the Reformed Blues Band, a pun on the name of the Dutch Reformed Church, in which most Afrikaans kids have had to do time at one stage or another. The name of the album was *Eet Kreef*, meaning "Eat Crayfish," a pun on Marie Antoinette's infamous utterance during the French Revolution: "Let them eat cake."

The whole movement was a tremendous hit with the media, as nothing new had happened in Afrikaans music for decades. Still regarded very much as the "language of the oppressor," Afrikaans was freed of this onerous tag in some way by the new wave. It was the first time that Afrikaans kids got up and sang about their disenchantment with the system that their forebears had created.

Says Kerkorrel:

"Of course you put yourself on the line if you are arrogant enough to stand up and to criticize. It's an arrogant thing to do, yet at this time in our history it seems so obvious there are certain things that just can't go on any more.

"We cannot have dignity as Afrikaners, as young Afrikaans people, unless we are willing to grant dignity to other people in this country.

"There is a democratic kraal. There are thousands of us. It's not just me and the small circle of people I work with. There's a gut feeling which is growing. Once the young Afrikaner says to the old: 'No, what you're doing is wrong,' it's final. The last sign.'"*

Early in 1989 Shifty organized the countrywide "Voelvry Toer" to promote the new Afrikaans music we had recorded. The tour aroused much controversy. It might be compared to the 1950s in America when rock and roll was emerging. The conservative establishment labeled the

*Interview with Adrienne Sichel, *The Star*, August 24, 1990.

music satanic and vulgar; if you played it backwards the devil spoke to you. There were also reports circulated that the perpetrators of the music drank blood, wore fetus earrings, and fornicated with animals. Really heavy stuff with no element of truth. The musicians were all intelligent Afrikaans kids who were concerned enough about the future of their country to get up and sing about its wrongs. The tour was banned from all Afrikaans campuses by the university authorities, but not without large-scale student demonstrations. It was nevertheless a huge success, receiving unprecedented media coverage for a musical event.

With all the forces ganged up against South African progressive music—the industry, government legislation, broadcasting authorities, conditioning, and so on—one would imagine that those producing alternative music would pull together and form a united front against such adversaries. However, because artist and company alike have so many hurdles to leap, harmony is not always easy to maintain, either between artists and Shifty or within the bands themselves. Universally, it seems, when business and art mix there is always some form of suspicion and mistrust, no matter what the history of the relationship.

It is difficult to be a noncommercial alternative record company in an industry in which those qualities are discouraged. It has meant that Shifty has often suffered from a shortage of manpower and financial backing. In addition, we have often acted as management and promoter as well as producer, and resources have been stretched to the limit. We have not always been able to promote an artist as effectively as we could have wished.

This situation adds to the deep frustration felt by artists who have chosen to stick to their principles and make music that they believe in, rather than sell out and make formula music that will get them on the radio and thus more easily afford them the chance to earn a secure living. A good many of these artists, who would certainly be able to survive ably in a healthy music scene, don't sell many records. Apart from the radio-play aspect, most bands still do not have management; promoters still have not taken up the challenge; and you can count the number of venues that will regularly stage this kind of music on one hand with a couple of fingers missing . . .

. . . but times are a-changing. Circumstances are altering fast in this country, and coincidentally there are perceptible signs of shifting attitudes in the greater music industry. Not so much from any newly gained altruistic vision, but more from the knowledge that with a changing South Africa come changing markets. Recently other companies have expressed interest in signing the kind of musician that previously only Shifty would have recorded. In 1990 three different distributors offered to take on our catalog. The number of records sold by Shifty artists has doubled every year since 1987. Also, some commercial artists are beginning to be a little more daring in what they say in their songs. These are all sure signs that our presence is being felt; it bodes well for the future development of a healthy music culture in South Africa.

The following Shifty Record albums are available in the U.S. from Rounder Records: "South African Trade Union Choirs"; "Forces Favorites"; and "Change is Pain" by Mzwakhe Mbuli. All other Shifty albums mentioned in this article, and the Shifty catalog, are available from: Shifty Records, Box 27513 Bertsham 2013, South Africa.

Glossary

ANC - African National Congress, an antigovernment group established in 1912 to seek equality for all races in South Africa

bantustan - "homeland" set aside for people defined by the South African government as "nonwhite"

Biko, Steve - anti-apartheid activist who died as a result of police brutality in 1977

doekie - headscarf

dominie - minister of the Dutch Reformed Church

Garvey, Marcus - West Indian Black leader, 1880-1940

imam - Muslim prayer leader

kaffir - abusive term for a Black South African

kettie - slingshot

kraal - pen for cattle or sheep

manumission - act of freeing from slavery

Pretoria - administrative capital of South Africa

rand - South African monetary unit

Shaka - founder of the Zulu Empire

sjambok - heavy leather whip

slaanver - type of weapon

veld - South African countryside

Bibliography

Breytenbach, Breyten. *The True Confessions of an Albino Terrorist*. London: Faber and Faber, 1984. The author, a White political prisoner in South Africa for seven years, writes of his time and torture while in jail.

Brink, André and J. M. Coetzee. *A Land Apart: A Contemporary South African Reader*. New York: Viking Penguin, 1987. A collection of writing by South Africans of various ethnic origins.

Finnegan, William. *Dateline Soweto: Travels with Black South African Reporters*. New York: Harper & Row, 1988. The author spent six weeks with journalists from the largest daily paper in South Africa, the Johannesburg *Star*, exploring their lives and their work.

Gordimer, Nadine. *The Essential Gesture: Writing, Politics and Places*. New York: Knopf, 1988. Essays, articles, and speeches by the South African writer covering the period 1959–1986. The book is a personal account of South Africa and apartheid in that time.

Gray, Stephen, ed. *Penguin Book of Southern African Verse*. New York: Penguin, 1989. A collection of works by South African poets.

Hirson, Denis. *The House Next Door to Africa*. Manchester: Carcanet, 1987. The saga of a family

Holland, Heidi. *The Struggle: A History of the African National Congress*. New York: Braziller, 1990. A history of the ANC, leading up to its legalization, written by a South African journalist.

Kitson, Norma. *Where Sixpence Lives*. Topsfield, MA: The Hogarth Press/Salem House, 1991. A powerful and disarming account of an anti–apartheid activist's struggle.

Malan, Rian. *My Traitor's Heart*. New York: The Atlantic Monthly Press, 1990. Malan, a South African exile, returns to the violence of his native land and faces his own experience as a White man in a nation ruled by apartheid.

Mathabane, Mark. *Kaffir Boy*. New York: Macmillan, 1986. The painful and moving autobiography of a Black South African born and raised in a "township."

Paton, Alan. *Cry, the Beloved Country*. New York: Charles Scribner's Sons, 1948. A highly acclaimed novel about a Zulu minister in South Africa whose family suffers greatly.

Russell, Diana E. H. *Lives of Courage: Women for a New South Africa*. New York: Basic Books, 1989. The South-African born sociologist interviewed women of diverse ethnicities.

Sampson, Anthony. *Black and Gold: Tycoons, Revolutionaries, and Apartheid*. New York: Pantheon, 1987. The author traces the history of the close and tragic relationship between business in South Africa and apartheid.

Serote, Mongane. *To Every Birth Its Blood*. New York: Thunder's Mouth Press, 1989. A novel concerning two journalists who realize that their lives mean little in the face of the enormous sacrifice required to end apartheid.

Stengel, Richard. *January Sun: One Day, Three Lives, A South African Town*. New York: Simon & Schuster, 1990. The author follows the lives of three men — an Afrikaner, a Black, and an Indian — through one day in their small town in the Transvaal.

Tessendorf, K. C. *Along the Road to Soweto: A Racial History of South Africa*. New York: Atheneum, 1989. An overview of the history of South African race relations.

Tillman, Iris and Alex Harris, eds. *Beyond the Barricades: Popular Resistance in South Africa*. New York: Aperture, 1989. Stunning photographs of South Africans and their struggle by twenty South African photographers.

Wicomb, Zoë. *You Can't Get Lost in Cape Town*. New York: Pantheon Books, 1987. A collection of stories about a Colored woman who returns to South Africa after living abroad.

Index